T0313603

SALVATORE BABONES

AMERICAN TIANXIA

Chinese money, American power,
and the end of history

POLICY PRESS SHORTS RESEARCH

First published in Great Britain in 2017 by

Policy Press
University of Bristol
1-9 Old Park Hill
Bristol
BS2 8BB
UK
t: +44 (0)117 954 5940
pp-info@bristol.ac.uk
www.policypress.co.uk

North America office:
Policy Press
c/o The University of Chicago Press
1427 East 60th Street
Chicago, IL 60637, USA
t: +1 773 702 7700
f: +1 773 702 9756
sales@press.uchicago.edu
www.press.uchicago.edu

© Policy Press 2017

British Library Cataloguing in Publication Data
A catalogue record for this book is available from the British Library.

Library of Congress Cataloging-in-Publication Data
A catalog record for this book has been requested.

ISBN 978-1-4473-3680-8 (hardcover)
ISBN 978-1-4473-3682-2 (ePub)
ISBN 978-1-4473-3683-9 (Mobi)
ISBN 978-1-4473-3681-5 (ePDF)

The right of Salvatore Babones to be identified as author of this work has been asserted by him in accordance with the Copyright, Designs and Patents Act 1988.

Cover design by Policy Press
Front cover: image kindly supplied by www.alamy.com
Printed and bound in Great Britain by CPI Group (UK) Ltd, Croydon, CR0 4YY
Policy Press uses environmentally responsible print partners

Contents

Preface

This short book tackles a big concept: *tianxia*, Chinese for "all under heaven." As China has come to play a major role in global affairs, Chinese scholars have resurrected this classical Confucian term to describe the kind of international system they would like to see: harmonious, ethical, relational, and (it literally goes without saying) centered on China. The classical Chinese *tianxia* was an East Asian world-system focused on one central state (China) to which all other peoples looked for legitimation and leadership. Today's millennial world-system is similarly focused on the United States. As the title of Chapter One says: right concept, wrong country.

The size of the US economy and its location at the center of the world-system has led to a merging of US and global systems of distinction: in almost every field, success in the world means success in the US, and vice versa. This is most true in business, where global value chains are overwhelmingly dominated by US companies, but it is true in most other fields as well. The result is that when Russian President Vladimir Putin complains of a world in which there is "one master, one sovereign" (the title of Chapter Two), it is not just the United States government that irks him. It is the entire American system, what might be called the American Tianxia.

Chinese President Xi Jinping is similarly unhappy to live in a US-centered world, but unlike Putin he has the resources to do something about it. That "something" is his "One Belt, One Road" initiative to link all of Afro-Eurasia into Chinese economic networks. The problem for Xi is that the countries that have most eagerly welcomed integration with China are too small and too poor to matter. Thus Chapter Three showcases one belt and one road to nowhere. Even China can't afford to purchase enough people's loyalties to set up an alternative global system, and the fact that it has to pay for what allies it has shows that the effort is unsustainable.

The American Tianxia is an extraordinarily stable world-system configuration. It is stable because the people of the world make it so – not the countries, the people. The United States was founded on individualism, and as more and more people put their individual interests ahead of those of their countries of birth, they come into alignment with the American Tianxia. Thus liberal individualism – not, pace Francis Fukuyama, liberal democracy – has emerged as the final ideology of freedom at Fukuyama's end of history. World-systems have a lifespan of centuries, so if history isn't exactly over, it will at least be in hiatus for several centuries (Chapter Four).

I first heard of the term *tianxia* at the end of 2015. I had spent several months working in the Wang Gungwu Library at the Chinese Heritage Centre (CHC) at Nanyang Technological University in Singapore. Prof. Wang Gungwu didn't donate the money for the library. He donated the books. As I later discovered, I had been reading "his" books all along. Reading through a great intellectual's library is surely an interesting way to learn: "ontogeny recapitulates phylogeny." When I finally met Prof. Wang himself at the CHC's twentieth anniversary gala, he suggested that I read his latest book, *Renewal: The Chinese State and the New Global History*.

The first chapter of the book introduces the *tianxia* concept, and a final 22-page appendix is entirely devoted to its intellectual history. They made no impression on me. Prof. Wang was, however, kind enough to meet me in his office at the National University of Singapore's East Asia Institute to discuss my thoughts on the structure of the world-economy. He mentioned that the *tianxia* concept might apply to the structure I was describing, and the proverbial lightbulb went on in my head. Sensing my enthusiasm, Prof. Wang immediately cautioned me that *tianxia* has and has had many different meanings in

Chinese. I told him not to worry, because henceforth it would have only one meaning in English.

I re-read *Renewal* that night, and having just finished *American Tianxia* I am re-reading it again right now. It is with great humility that I dedicate this book to Prof. Wang, and I am grateful that he has allowed me to do so. Whether or not he agrees with its arguments, he inspired them. Without his library, his intellectual generosity, and most of all his encouragement this book would never have been written. Now that it has been written, I hope it proves worthy of the dedication.

Salvatore Babones
February 28, 2017
Sydney

1

Right concept, wrong country

The rise of China in the wake of the slow relative decline of the United States has been the overarching narrative of global studies since the beginning of this century. Is this narrative correct? China's growth is slowing as it reaches middle income status and the United States is still overwhelmingly more wealthy and powerful than China. If China will someday "overtake" the United States, it will not happen for decades or centuries, depending on what is meant by overtaking. But even this more guarded account of US decline is colored by an outdated, state-centric view of human society. The twenty-first century world-system is centered on the United States but not contained within it; individuals all over the world participate in hierarchies of distinction that are fundamentally American in ideology and orientation. Whether or not they agree with US policy, support the US president, or are even able to enter the United States, success-oriented individuals choose to live in an American world – or accept global social exclusion. This is just as true in China as anywhere else, and perhaps even more true for Chinese individuals than for anyone else.

From the dawn of history until the long sixteenth century, China was the economic, political, and cultural center of East Asia. It was arguably the most important economic center in the world. East Asia was distinctive in having one center. Other regions of the world had centers that were vigorously contested or that shifted over time. For example, for most of its history the Indian subcontinent has had no one dominant center; power and influence shifted from state to state with no one state being consistently accepted as the central state of the region. Similarly the Valley of Mexico seems to have come to be dominated by the Aztecs only shortly before the arrival of the Spanish conquistadors. Tracking the center of Western civilization is even more difficult. Traditional histories of the Western world begin in Egypt and Mesopotamia, after which the center of what is teleologically known as the "West" shifts ever westward, first to Greece, then to Rome, then to France, England, and ultimately the United States. In most of the world, centers rise, fall, shift, and rise again. But not in East Asia.

In East Asia, at least in East Asia before the intrusion of Europeans, things were different. From long before the beginning of the written historical record, East Asia was centered on China. Contemporary China is the lineal descendant of a civilization that stretches back at least 4000 years and has always existed in situ where it still exists today. The Chinese writing system has been in continuous use for more than 3000 years and "is the only originally invented writing system still in use today" (Kern, 2010, p. 1). More importantly from a systems perspective, it is still being used in the same geographical space by people who identify themselves as being of the same culture – and indeed of the same race – as its prehistoric inventors. China was first unified politically in 221 BC by the Qin Emperor (r. 221-210 BC) but it was a single political space at least a thousand years before that. When Confucius wandered from state to state in the early fifth century BC offering (mostly unwanted) advice on how to rule in a just manner, he understood China as a single political system and his patrons as participants in that system.

The Chinese people and the Chinese language have long recognized the coherence of China as a unified political system, even if China has often been divided into multiple warring polities. The name the Chinese give to their own country is *Zhongguo*. The word is literally translatable as "Central State" or "Central States" (there is no plural inflection in Chinese). It is more evocatively translated into English as "Middle Kingdom." China is not the land of the Chin (as it is in English, referring to the Qin Emperor) or the land of the Han (the majority ethnic group of China). It is simply and matter-of-factly the central state or states in the same self-evident way that for the Greco-Roman world the Mediterranean was the middle sea. It didn't need a proper name of its own.

By the time of the classical Han Dynasty (206 BC-AD 220) Chinese geographers were already well-aware that the world was much bigger than just China. Of course they knew about their immediate neighbors in East Asia, Southeast Asia, and Central Asia. But by the first century AD they also knew about the Roman Empire, which they honorifically called *Daqin* (the Great Qin), putting it on a par with China itself (Yu, 1986, p. 379). Buddhism was established in China around this time (Demieville, 1986, p. 821), implying some knowledge of India, and in the second century AD the Chinese imperial government unsuccessfully attempted to open a trade route to India via Yunnan (Yu, 1986, p. 458). Starting in the fifth century AD Chinese Buddhists made regular pilgrimages to South and Southeast Asia (Wang, 1959, pp. 2-3). Thus throughout the subsequent development of Chinese political thought, Chinese scholars had access to at least a basic understanding of Asian political geography.

Unlike classical and medieval Western geography, which always placed its own civilization on the northwestern edge of the known world, Chinese geography has always located China in the middle (Callahan, 2012, p. 629). The traditional Chinese "Five Zone" theory organized the Chinese world into concentric circles: first the royal domain of lands under the personal lordship of the emperor, then the domains of the emperor's Chinese subsidiary lords, and then the conquered kingdoms of non-Chinese peoples, the internal barbarians (these three zones being inside the Chinese empire itself). Outside these three civilized zones were the tributary barbarians, who sent customary tribute to the emperor's court as a token of submission, and the "wild" barbarians, who did not (Yu, 1986, pp. 379-380). The first three zones were in theory subject to Chinese law, while countries in the two outer zones were free to live according to their own customs.

The five zones taken together formed the Chinese *tianxia* (literally "sky beneath," idiomatically "all under heaven").

The concept of *tianxia* has existed throughout Chinese history but its meaning and implications have shifted over the centuries. Originally applied to encompass the literal whole world (Qi and Shen, 2015, pp. 273-274), early on it came to represent "an enlightened realm that Confucian thinkers and mandarins raised to one of universal values that determined who was civilized and who was not" (Wang, 2013, p. 133). The term encompassed "China and her neighboring polities" and "implied a world order in which the king of China ruled [China] directly and ... neighboring regions of China ... indirectly" (Chang, 2011, p. 34). The most influential living Chinese philosopher of the *tianxia* concept describes it as operating on three levels: "(1) the earth or all lands under the sky ... (2) a common or public choice made by all peoples in the world, truly representing the general will ... and (3) a universal political system for the world" (Zhao, 2012, p. 59).

When Zhao, an ethicist, writes "the world" he means the entire world as we know it today, but of course the historical Chinese usage of *tianxia* applied the term to the world as it was known at the relevant time of use: that is, to the Chinese world. It referred to the political system of which China was the central state (or states), not to the geographical world, which might extend to such remote and exotic places as the Roman Empire. The historical Chinese *tianxia* corresponded, roughly speaking, to East Asia and the adjacent regions of Central Asia, a region in which China was (and is again) by far the economically, politically, and culturally preponderant country. From the apparently prehistoric emergence of a common Chinese consciousness until the crisis of January 7, 1841, when a single British ship sank an entire Chinese fleet in less than four hours (Hoe and Roebuck, 1999, p. 149), China was the central state (or states) of the East Asian political system. It was perceived as such by the leaders of neighboring countries (Jiang, 2011, 105).

The Chinese *tianxia* before the industrial revolution was "an almost closed 'international' socioeconomic system" so dominated by China that "the Chinese state was not a state at all in the conventional meaning of the word, but rather the administration of civilized society *in toto*" (Mancall, 1971, pp. 7 and 3, italics in original). That sense of the Chinese *tianxia* as the sum total of the civilized world survived the arrival of Europeans by sea in the sixteenth century and by land in the seventeenth. It still survives to some extent today.

As suggested by the famous opening line of the classic Chinese epic *The Romance of the Three Kingdoms*, China has not always been united as a single state: "The empire, long divided, must unite; long united, must divide." China has often been a multitude of states, as it was in the time of Confucius himself. During such times princes vied for the *tianming* (literally "heavenly mandate," or "mandate of heaven"), a quality demonstrated by righteousness and benevolence – or more realistically, by battlefield success. China has also fallen under non-Chinese rule, as under the Mongol Yuan Dynasty (AD 1271-1368) and the Manchurian Qing Dynasty (AD 1644-1911). But when Mongols and Manchurians conquered China, they did not rule it from their previous domains. They assumed the *tianming* and ruled their former homes from the center, as emperors of China. Thus whether united under Chinese rule, disunited, or ruled by outsiders, China was always at the center of its world.

The *tianxia* revival

The moral dimension of *tianxia* as a conceptualization of China's place in the world and *tianming* as the right to rule it is deeply rooted in the traditional Confucian concept of *datong* ("great harmony"). *Datong* makes its first appearance in the *Book of Rites*, one of the five canonical texts of classical Confucianism. It represents a kind of prelapsarian golden age during which people cared for all of humanity as they did their own parents and children (Bell, 2008, p. 23). In the early 2000s, this Confucian ideal of harmony began to replace Marxian class struggle as the guiding principle of Chinese official rhetoric (Callahan, 2004, p. 574). The revival of the Confucian concept of *datong* either inspired or was inspired by Chinese President Hu Jintao's "Harmonious Society" slogan. In his 2006 Central Committee speech outlining the principles of the "Harmonious Society," Hu claimed that *datong* resulted from the fulfillment of the socialist promise of "from each according to his ability, to each according to his need" (Mahoney, 2008, p. 115), an attempted sleight of hand that can be seen as a transparent effort to legitimize rampant inequality by reference to Confucian principles.

The *datong* ideal also found a foreign policy application in the relationship between *datong* and *tianxia*. In a 2005 speech to the United Nations, Hu advanced the doctrine of the "Harmonious World" as China's approach to international relations. Though he did not mention the Confucian *tianxia* concept directly, it is widely understood that *tianxia* incorporates "the idea of 'great harmony' [*datong*] at a much higher level" (Luo, 2008, p. 102), i.e., that of the world taken as a whole (see also Huang and Shih, 2014, pp. 157-161). In other words, *tianxia* does not merely denote a worldwide political system in the way that *zhongguo* merely denotes the central state or states of a system. *Tianxia* also implies a moral component: as Wang (2013, p. 133) puts it, *tianxia* is "an abstract notion embodying the idea of a superior moral authority." Germany is self-evidently the *zhongguo* (to use the term metaphorically) of Europe, but a Europe united under Nazi dictatorship could never have been a German *tianxia*.

In line with Hu's emphasis on harmony, Zhao Tingyang laid out a contemporary model for a morally-grounded, harmonious global *tianxia* in his best-selling 2005 book *The Tianxia System* (available in Chinese only; see Zhang, 2010 for publication details and a review). In an article-length summary of his argument, he characterizes this new approach as the creation of "a world under a commonly agreed institution, a plan to make the world a place of world-ness" (Zhao, 2006, p. 34). In Zhao's model (as in Hu's United Nations speech) the desired global *tianxia* would be non-hierarchical, and there is no suggestion that it would be centered on China. Instead there is a pure globalism that has no geographical specificity:

> All-under-Heaven [*tianxia*] ... means an institutionally ordered world or a world institution responsible to confirm the political

legitimacy of world governance as well as local governance, and to allow the justification of systems. (Zhao, 2006, p. 39)

Zhao explicitly clothes his global *tianxia* in the Hu-friendly rhetoric of harmony:

> Beyond the concepts of war and peace, "harmony" seeks reasonable resolutions of conflicts and stable security by building truly reliable correlations of mutual benefit in the long run, as well as reciprocal acceptance of the other's values. (Zhao, 2012, p. 48)

Bell (2008, p. 26) argues that Zhao's goal of universal harmony is "radically inconsistent with key [hierarchical] Confucian values" but Zhao himself draws extensively on Confucian thought and is widely regarded as a Confucian revivalist. Zhao reconciles Confucianism with "reciprocal acceptance" by replacing the conventional idea of "uniform universalism" with his own brand of "compatible universalism" (Zhao, 2012, pp. 62-63). For Zhao, uniform universalism is the globalization of Western world society theory (Meyer et al., 1997), in which all peoples of the world are seen to be converging toward a single, shared value system. Zhao is particularly scathing of what he perceives to be the individualism of uniform universalism. Zhao's compatible universalism, by contrast, is relational, and depends on mutual tolerance and the prioritization of the maintenance of relationships over the rights of individuals.

Zhao's focus on relational values and dismissal of individualism are echoed by Chinese political scientist Qin Yaqing's normative theory of relational governance. Qin defines relational governance as:

> a process of negotiating socio-political arrangements that manage complex relationships in a community to produce order so that members behave in a reciprocal and cooperative fashion with mutual trust evolved over a shared understanding of social norms and human morality. (Qin, 2011, p. 133)

Qin derives the principle of relational governance from the classic Confucian dialectic of *yin* and *yang*, which he views "as being fundamentally harmonious; the interaction between them is the process of harmonisation" (Qin, 2012, p. 81). Comparing his relational governance concept to Zhao's *tianxia* approach, Qin (2012, p. 85) judges Zhao to be much more ambitious. Qin offers a relational framework for state-to-state relations, whereas Zhao implicitly advocates the dissolution of states into a kind of global commonwealth. On the surface, Zhao and Qin seem to offer competing blueprints of how the human world should operate. Nonetheless, they share a foundation in classical Confucianism (for Zhao, the *Book of Rites*; for Qin, the *Book of Changes*), a focus on relationality, and (unsurprisingly) an affinity with Hu Jintao's "Harmonious World." Both rely on the family metaphor, contrasting a supposed Chinese emphasis on the family with a supposed Western emphasis on the individual. They share with Hu a vision of the world as one big happy family – implicitly assuming that all families, or at least all Confucian families, are happy, or at least harmonious.

Zhao (2009, 2012) somewhat fantastically grounds his conceptual models in an analysis of interstate (or inter-fiefdom) relationships under China's legendary Zhou Dynasty (1046-256 BC), the political system in which Confucius himself lived. It is thus safe to say that his empirical assertions can be taken with a grain of salt. Qin is much more practical but equally fantastical: he portrays contemporary East Asia as a successful example of relational governance based on shared Confucian values. He claims that "regional cooperation and governance has been quite a fact in the region," exemplified by the fact that "China has so far established more than 40 'partnerships' of various kinds that include almost all major players, nation-states, and regional actors" (Qin, 2011, p. 144). He contrasts the cozy family atmosphere of East Asia with the individualistic, rules-based environment of the European Union. This may be even less convincing than lessons drawn from the Zhou Dynasty.

Interestingly, neither Zhao nor Qin chooses to illustrate compatible universalism or relational governance using the one obvious empirical case from Chinese history: the well-documented Ming Dynasty (AD 1368-1644). The Ming Dynasty should have been the obvious case for Zhao because it self-consciously adopted the *tianxia* principle in organizing its internal and international relations; for Qin, because it understood its relations with the dangerous "wild" or outer barbarians explicitly in terms of the tension between *yin* (the dark ignorance of the barbarians) and *yang* (the civilizational light of China) (Jiang, 2011, pp. 103-107). The early Ming Dynasty was resolutely Confucian in rhetoric and to a great extent in reality. One of the first acts of the first Ming Emperor (the Hongwu Emperor, r. 1368-1398) was to establish a national, state-funded network of schools for the teaching of the Confucian classics (Hucker, 1998, p. 31).

The Ming Dynasty's Confucianism, embodied in the Great Ming Code, was universal, but not uniform, in application (non-Chinese peoples were not expected to conform to Chinese customs), and most disputes between neighboring states within the Ming *tianxia* were settled on relational terms, via negotiation. Immediately after winning the throne, the Hongwu Emperor sent emissaries to the rulers of China's main vassal states, stressing his intention to return to the traditional rituals of symbolic recognition following a century of more nakedly threatening orders from Mongol Yuan Dynasty (Wang, 1998, p. 303). His resumption of Confucian tradition was apparently well-received, at least in the court of China's closest neighbor and tributary, Korea (Zhang, 2015a, p. 51). Throughout his reign the Hongwu Emperor worked to consolidate, rather than expand, his empire, and along those lines he advised his successors:

> The overseas foreign countries ... are separated from us by mountains and seas and far away in a corner. [...] If they were so unrealistic as to disturb our borders, it would be unfortunate for them. If they gave us no trouble and we moved troops to fight them unnecessarily, it would be unfortunate for us. I am concerned that future generations might abuse China's wealth and power and covet the military glories of the moment to send armies into the field without reason and cause a loss of life. May

they be sharply reminded that this is forbidden. (Wang, 1998, pp. 311-312)

One author who does draw the obvious connection between Chinese relational theory and the international relations of the Ming Dynasty is Feng Zhang. In a book-length treatment, Zhang (2015a) tests relational theory against early Ming China's foreign relations with Korea, Japan, and Mongolia. He explicitly references both Zhao and Qin as inspirations for his study. Piercing the familial facade of Confucian international relations, Zhang (pp. 26-27) divides the motives behind relational strategies into instrumental (realist) and expressive (communitarian) rationalities. He finds that over the course of the early Ming period (1368-1424) instrumental approaches were dominant 79 percent of the time and expressive approaches the remaining 21 percent (p. 177). But around two-thirds of Zhang's expressive cases are characterized by what he calls "expressive hierarchy" – i.e., Confucian solidarity of the type that emphasizes "the propriety of [the] serving [of] the great by the small" (p. 160). Apparently the Chinese Foreign Minister Yang Jiechi shared this understanding when in 2010 he notoriously told his Singaporean counterpart that "China is a big country and other countries are small countries, and that's just a fact." No wonder Hu, Zhao, and Qin steer clear of the Ming example.

Hierarchy and peace

The Ming Dynasty *tianxia* might not have been as harmonious as China's twenty-first century Confucians might have liked, though Zhang (2015a, pp. 181-183) puts a brave face on things by claiming that relationalism can potentially be purged of its hierarchical tendencies. Nonetheless the Ming *tianxia* does seem to have been relatively peaceful, especially when compared to similar periods in European history, or indeed pre-Mughal India or pre-Columbian Mexico. Kang (2010) identifies only four major international wars during the three centuries of Ming rule among the states that were subject to the Ming tributary system, and the last of those wars hardly counts, considering that it was the one that brought the system to an end. Kang is certainly overstating the peacefulness of the system by classifying away many lower-level conflicts (Purdue, 2015, pp. 1005 and 1008). Nonetheless, his argument is not without merit. Just one major war per century is surely a record to be envied, however many minor wars may have continued to be fought year in and year out. But should this record of major power peace be attributed to the relationalism of the Ming *tianxia*, or to its hierarchy?

Our own era may seem to be one of endless warfare, but when you take a step back to look at the data it is in fact remarkably peaceful. Pinker (2011) and Morris (2014) argue that armed conflict is at an all-time low, in the literal sense of all of human history. More strikingly, since 1945 there has not been a single major, internationally-recognized change in the international borders between the countries of the world that resulted from warfare. In the decolonization of the mid-twentieth century many internal borders became international borders, a process repeated again with the breakup of the Soviet Union, Yugoslavia, and Czechoslovakia in the early 1990s. Sometimes these processes of disintegration were characterized by terrible violence, as in the partitions of India and Yugoslavia, and several former Portuguese colonies were violently seized by post-colonial countries (Goa, East Timor). Many countries have also experienced and are experiencing civil wars. But outright wars between countries on the model of the previous 3000 years of human political history have been rare, and when they have occurred the most common outcome has been a return to the pre-war borders. The right of conquest seems to be a thing of the past.

There are limited exceptions that prove the general rule, most prominently the Israeli annexation of East Jerusalem in 1967 and the Russian annexation of Crimea in 2014. Neither of these annexations has received widespread international recognition. This might be credited to the new institutionalism in international relations, were it not for the fact that illegal, de facto annexations are also rare. East Jerusalem and Crimea are exceptions, not the rule. The rule seems to be that countries don't invade other countries anymore, and when they do invade other countries they do so with limited objectives and withdraw to the pre-war borders once those objectives have been met. Sometimes they maintain an open-ended state of uncertainty, as exemplified by Russia's many frozen conflicts with its neighbors. But *veni, vidi, vici* seems to be a thing of the past. Among Western developed countries, including the United States, the whole idea of using military power to conquer adjoining territories is considered mad.

Which is not to deny that the United States uses military power. It uses military power frequently, but it does not use its power in conventionally Westphalian ways. International relations scholars use the 1648 Peace of Westphalia that ended the Thirty Years' War in central Europe to mark the transition from feudalism to the modern system of state sovereignty. The Treaty of Westphalia itself did not mention sovereignty or lay out rules for international relations, but what we now call the Westphalian system of state sovereignty emerged out of the norms and practices of European interstate relations after the Peace of Westphalia (Croxton, 1999). For example, the systematic exchange of resident ambassadors employed in permanent embassies started in this period (Wheaton, 1836, p. 167). In the modern interstate system that was born in Europe around 1648, states routinely used military power to acquire territory, whether to extend the frontiers of their own countries, to establish settler colonies of their own citizens, or to impose exploitative colonial rule over foreigners. Not any more.

It is ironic that just as the United States became the most powerful country in the world, it stopped using its military power to acquire territory. The United States repeatedly used force throughout the nineteenth century to extend its frontiers across North America to the Pacific Ocean, to establish a settler colony on Hawaii in the 1890s, and finally to seize its first colonial possessions in the Spanish–American War of 1898. And then it stopped. At the Paris Peace Conference that followed the end of World War I, the United States was perhaps the only country that did not press claims for the expansion (or preservation) of its territory. The Treaty of Versailles is often portrayed as a failure because it did not prevent the rise of fascism and the outbreak of World War II. But considering that the

United States hardly registered as a European power a mere 10 years before, it should perhaps be reappraised as a substantial US diplomatic accomplishment.

The historical memory of World War I has come to be so overshadowed by the tragedies and triumphs of World War II that it is difficult to remember now just how dominant the United States was then. Figure 1.1 uses gross domestic product (GDP) per capita and population estimates from the widely-used Angus Maddison cliometric database (Bolt and van Zanden, 2014) to calculate total GDP for five of the world's most powerful countries of the first half of the twentieth century. At the signing of the Treaty of Versailles in 1919 the GDP of the United States was equal to that of the United Kingdom, Germany, Russia, and Japan combined. Despite the enormous physical size of the British and French empires, contemporaries were well-aware that the United States pulled the strings that mattered in global affairs, particularly the financial strings. The American historian Charles Beard told an amusing though sadly unsourced anecdote about this, quoting "a keen French economist" as saying:

> One fact dominates all others: the rise of the United States to world hegemony. Lord Robert Cecil [architect of the League of Nations] has compared the position of the United States after the Great War with that of Great Britain after the Napoleonic wars. That comparison is not quite exact; because the British hegemony was then essentially European while that of the United States today is universal. (Beard, 1922, pp. 243–244)

This is not mere American swagger. The British philosophers Bertrand and Dora Russell agreed. Regarding the future of relations between the United States and the United Kingdom, they reasoned that:

> one of two things must happen, either an alliance in which the British Empire would take second place, or a war in which the British Empire would be dissolved. An alliance would only be possible if we sincerely abandoned all furtherance of our own

imperialism and all opposition to that of America. If this should happen, an English-speaking block could very largely control the world, and make first-class wars improbable during its existence. (Russell and Russell, 1923, p. 69)

Russell and Russell's mooted Anglo-American alliance was not forthcoming at the time, with the result that several more "first-class wars" were fought, culminating in World War II. Even after World War II, the United Kingdom did not "sincerely abandon all furtherance of its own imperialism" and subordinate its foreign policy to the imperative of maintaining its "special relationship" with the United States until after the Suez Crisis of 1956. Half a century later, the United Kingdom and its Anglo-Saxon former dominions (Canada, Australia, and New Zealand) are extraordinarily well-integrated into American power structures, especially military ones (Babones, 2015a, p. 59). The Reagan–Thatcher alliance has been credited with bringing about the fall of the Soviet Union (O'Sullivan, 2006), and whether or not that is an overstatement it is clearly true that there have been no "first-class wars" since the solidification of the Anglo-Saxon alliance system half a century ago.

Figure 1.1: Comparison of US and other countries' GDP (2016 dollars), 1900–1950

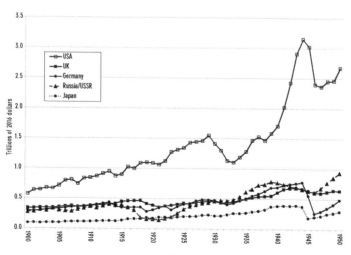

Toward an American Tianxia

Like the United States in the early twentieth century, the United Kingdom after the middle of the twentieth century ceased to use force to impose its rule on foreigners. Most of the rest of the world followed suit. It is surely intriguing that when France withdrew from Vietnam in 1954, the United States did not take over its colonial occupation. However misguided the US involvement in Vietnam may have been, it was a war to support one indigenous regime over another, not a war to impose a US regime. This is typical of the use of US power since 1900 and absolutely characteristic of the use of US power since 1950: the United States uses military force to influence modes of governance within countries, not to change the borders of countries. The American global order is a status quo order with respect to countries' international borders but an interventionist order with respect to countries' internal affairs. This is a radically post-Westphalian approach to international relations (Babones, 2017a).

The definitive principle of modern Westphalian sovereignty was non-interference in the internal affairs of countries (Krasner, 1999), a principle still aggressively asserted by Chinese and Russian leaders and intellectuals. This principle, though never absolute, is now absolutely defunct. In the post-war period the United States and the Soviet Union repeatedly asserted a right to interfere in the internal affairs of their allies and associates, in effect waging a global proxy war for influence within the borders of other countries. Since the dissolution of the Soviet Union in 1991 the United States has been the only serious force ordering the internal affairs of other countries on a global scale. Russia attempts to do so, but with limited success and mainly inside the borders of the former Soviet Union. Russia's only major "out of area" operation since 1991 has been its intervention in the Syrian civil war, and even Syria is a country where Russia still possesses Soviet-era military bases. The United States, by contrast, has deep civil and military relationships on every continent, including permanent military facilities in at least 70 countries (Vine, 2015, pp. 3-4).

These US relationships are instrumental with some partners and expressive with others, to use Zhang's (2015a) categories. The deep relationship between the United States and Saudi Arabia's repressively theocratic oil monarchy is clearly instrumental. But the relationships between the United States and its four Anglo-Saxon allies are equally clearly expressive. The same is true not only for NATO allies but for the West as a whole. Countries like Sweden and Switzerland may not be members of NATO, but no one doubts that their states and societies are firmly aligned with those of the United States, not Russia or China. One might even say that the West as a whole is tied together by what Zhang (2015a, p. 181) calls "ethical relationalism," a system in which "the most proper ends are not exclusive self-interest, but sustainable long-term ethical relationships." The one caveat to this interpretation is that though most peer-to-peer relationships within the West may be characterized as purely ethical (e.g., German solidarity with Canada), relationships between individual Western countries and the United States are unavoidably hierarchical. As Khong (2013, p. 17) remarks with regard to the principle of the sovereign equality of states, "few would presume to deal with the United States as an equal."

The remarkable stability of international borders since the middle of the twentieth century, coupled with the shredding of the Westphalian principle of non-interference in internal affairs, suggests that some powerful overarching force is ordering and stabilizing the contemporary world-system. When it is observed that the United States alone possesses such powerful overarching force, and frequently uses it, the case is complete. Just as China has always been the central state of East Asia, the United States is today the central state of the world. That doesn't mean that the United States dictates the actions of every country in the world. But it does mean that most of the countries of the world accede to American global leadership, both in their rhetoric and in their actions (Khong, 2013, pp. 37–39). Khong (2013) calls this the "American Tributary System" by explicit comparison to the Ming Dynasty tributary system, but a better term might be the "American Tianxia." The eminent historian Wang Gungwu was the first to suggest that:

> Today ... an American *tianxia* has a strong global presence. It has a missionary drive that is backed by unmatched military power and political influence. Compared to the Chinese concept, it is not passive and defensive; rather, unlike other universal ideals, it is supported by a greater capacity to expand. (Wang, 2013, p. 135)

The American Tianxia is not a tributary system on the Chinese model, only larger. It is, as Wang suggests, a new form of *tianxia*, a new ethical system for awarding distinction in virtually every field of human endeavor and ultimately for defining civilization itself. When Khong (2013) compares contemporary US international relations to those of Ming China, he focuses on only one aspect of the American Tianxia: state-to-state relations. But in the contemporary world-system, distinction hierarchies of all kinds find their summits in the United States. Those peaks may be in New York (media, finance, art, fashion, publishing, philanthropy, etc.), Boston (education), Silicon Valley (information technology), Hollywood (film), or even Baltimore (medicine), but they all represent a merging of American and global distinction hierarchies. Nowhere is this clearer than in business. Across 25 broad global industry sectors, US firms earn the highest profit share in 18 (Starrs, 2013, pp. 822–823). Despite a similarly large home market, Chinese firms lead in two – banking (in China, entirely state-owned) and construction (no surprise there) – with Hong Kong taking first place in real estate development. In field after field, success in the world means success in the United States, and vice versa.

There are many centers of excellence in specific fields scattered all around the world, but in nearly every field aside from sports the preponderance of peak institutions are fundamentally American institutions. When peak organizations are not actually based in the United States or staffed by citizens of the United States, they are strongly influenced by American organizational models, seek recognition from American governing bodies, run on American software, and conduct business in English. This places a heavy handicap on all non-American organizations and individuals with ambitions to succeed on the global stage, a handicap weighed in direct proportion to the organization's or individual's cultural and political distance from the United States. English-speaking Canadians pay a small price to participate in American/global distinction hierarchies, Italians somewhat more so, Russians much more, and Chinese most of all. American individuals, organizations, and institutions reap the rewards.

The American Tianxia is, in essence, a graded global club that people can join only if they behave in civilizationally-appropriate ways – and then pay a membership fee to boot. Proposals abound for the formation of alternative clubs, but the network externalities of joining the American club are so enormous that few people choose instead to join the Russian and Chinese clubs, despite their much lower membership fees. Even many elite Russians and Chinese prefer membership in the American club to membership in their own. Americans, of course, get in free – not just to their own club, but to most others as well. More than that, they are often paid to join. It is well-established that US foreign direct investment abroad systematically earns higher returns than foreigners' investments in the United States (Curcuru et al., 2013). It seems likely that a similar (if less easily measured) "exorbitant privilege" prevails in other fields as well. Simply put, Americans living in an American Tianxia don't have to work as hard as everyone else. When it's time to pay the piper, the piper pays them.

2

One master, one sovereign

The continuing resilience of the US economy is one of the great mysteries of international economics. The United States has consistently run a current account deficit for decades, averaging 2.9 percent of GDP over the period 1985-2015 (World Bank, 2016). For any ordinary country this would be a sign of impending economic catastrophe. Compounding the mystery is the fact that the United States has an enormously negative level of net international investment: foreigners hold several trillion dollars more in US assets than US entities hold in assets abroad (Curcuru et al., 2013, p. 2). Alarmist headlines about massive trade deficits and the selling off of America are, strictly speaking, correct. Yet the US continues to have by far the highest GDP per capita of any large economy, the US economy continues to grow at a steady rate, and there are no indications that investors expect an imminent collapse of the US economy (Babones, 2017b). The yield on 30-year US government bonds, a standard indicator of long-term risk expectations, has been on a steady downward trend for the last 30 years (FRED, 2017).

The seemingly dire structural deficits that characterize the US economy are balanced by a series of economic rents that can be characterized as a modern form of tribute. Many of these rents are directly related to the central status of the US dollar in the world's financial system. In a major review of the literatures on dollar rents, McCauley (2015) summarizes them as deriving from (1) the fact that the US borrows in its own currency, (2) foreign holdings of physical US currency, (3) the use of the dollar as a reserve currency, (4) the excess returns earned by US investments abroad compared to foreign investments in the US, and (5) advantages enjoyed by US banks in global finance.

McCauley acknowledges the existence of all of these rents but is skeptical about their aggregate value. What he may be missing – and what no straightforward econometric analysis can measure – are the positive externalities generated by putting all of these advantages together. Externalities are spillover effects generated by actions that are taken for some other purpose. They are a form of unintended consequence. The American Tianxia thrives on positive externalities. For example, are leading US investment banks able to leverage dollar rents to gain a disproportionate share of securities underwriting business in Asia? Do US management consulting and public relations firms piggy-back on the banks' business? Do Chinese people who have experience working in these US firms have an advantage on the Chinese job market? Are their parents thus willing to pay a premium to acquire a US education for their children that might gain them entry into these firms? The opportunities for such externalities are as real as they are endless.

The fact that American organizations and individuals systematically benefit from positive externalities generated by the rational behavior of non-American institutions and individuals is the economic foundation of the American Tianxia. It is what makes the American Tianxia self-sustaining and expansionary. It is tempting to characterize the continuous, voluntary transfer of money and power to American institutions as a form of tribute on the classical Chinese model. This is not, however, how international relations scholars understand the world. Khong (2013, p. 6) characterizes "the United States as the hub or epicenter of a tributary system analogous to that of China's during the Ming and Qing dynasties," but like other political scientists he understands the tributary system primarily in terms of diplomatic recognition (Zhang, 2009; Zhang and Buzan, 2012). Yet the Chinese tributary system was also a highly-regulated economic system for managing international trade (Jiang, 2011, pp. 118-123).

Though Ming Chinese and contemporary American business practices are light-years apart, from a structural standpoint the main difference between them is that whereas Chinese tributary trade operated on a strict top-down basis, today's American tributary system is very much a bottom-up affair. Ming China actively sought to suppress private trade, with the government sometimes going so far as to buy up the privately imported goods that were sent along with foreign tributary missions at a premium to market prices (Zhang, 2015a, pp. 166-167). Of course, private foreign investment was practically speaking non-existent. Ming China nominally prohibited Chinese traders from leaving the country, and those who were caught attempting to leave the country faced death by strangulation (Jiang, 2011, pp. 118 and 112-113). Today international trade is widespread, foreign direct investment is highly coveted, and economic immigration is common.

As a result of its bottom-up foundations, the American Tianxia is much more deeply ingrained in system-wide economic hierarchies than was the Ming *tianxia* in East Asia six centuries ago. The Ming *tianxia* was clearly hierarchical, but Wang (1968, p. 61) suggests that it can more accurately be understood in terms of "the principle of superiority together with that of security or inviolability." The American Tianxia admits no such principle of inviolability. All countries, friends and foes alike, are penetrated by global distinction hierarchies that support the extraction of American tributary rents. The only question is whether they are penetrated or permeated. The direction of hierarchy is clear.

Some of the structural factors that differentiate the historical Ming tianxia and the contemporary American Tianxia are summarized in the top half of Table 2.1. First, while the Ming *tianxia* was emphatically Confucian in ideology, the defining ideology of the American Tianxia is individualism. But individualism is an empty container. Liberal principles like human rights, democracy, and rule of law have evolved into a superstructure that elaborates and maintains the base principle of the primacy of the individual, but they have no specific content in themselves (i.e., what policies should democracies pursue? what should people do with their freedoms? what objectives should laws seek to accomplish?). All that is very different from Confucianism. Confucianism prescribed an extensive set of specific policies, actions, and objectives, particularly in its Ming-era neo-Confucian distillation. The American-style "pursuit of happiness" does not simply offer an alternative set of cultural expectations, like Indian Brahmanism or medieval European Christianity. American individualism is the ideology of the empty set: individualism is the ideology that has no tenets.

Table 2.1: Comparison of the Ming *tianxia* and the American Tianxia

Dimension		Ming *tianxia*	American Tianxia
Ideology		Confucianism	Individualism
Network type		State-to-state relations	Individual embeddedness
Stance		Defensive	Expansionary
Acquiescence		Mandatory	Voluntary
Surplus flow		Outward	Inward
Human flow		Outward	Inward
Five zones	Internal	Royal domain	DC–NY–Boston axis
		Subsidiary domains	Remainder of United States
		Internal barbarians	Anglo-Saxon allies
	External	Tributary barbarians	Other allies and aligned states
		"Wild" barbarians	Nonaligned states and enemies

Individualism means that even when countries have hostile relations with the United States, their citizens can still attend US universities, work in US companies, and (if they want) hope to become US citizens. Ming China used state-to-state relations to defend its society against foreign influences; American institutions self-consciously use people-to-people relationships as a tool for changing values in other societies. This appeal to individuals rather than states generates the ironic contradiction that the American Tianxia is inexorably expansionary while nonetheless maintaining a voluntary approach to the recruitment of new adherents. The United States, its corporations, its universities, and its NGOs are remarkably successful in exporting liberal values by offering individuals opportunities for personal self-advancement. Chinese elites can realistically aspire to attend US universities and work in US companies if they are willing to embrace an individualistic mindset. If they don't conform, they won't succeed, but that is their choice. This appeal to self-interest is an incredibly powerful recruitment tool. By contrast, in those rare instances when the United States has sought to impose liberal values by force (e.g., Afghanistan, Iraq), it has failed spectacularly.

In the Ming *tianxia*, both economic surplus and economic actors seem to have leaked out of the center, toward the peripheries. The evidence for this is circumstantial but one-sided. First, experts agree that the early Ming tributary trade generally benefited the tributary (Khong, 2013, p. 12). The emperor was able to demonstrate his superior status by bestowing gifts of visibly greater value than those he received in tribute from his vassals, and as a result the imperial court was never very concerned to promote tributary trade (Tsiang, 1936, pp. 34, quoted in Fairbank and Teng, 1942, p. 140). Quite the contrary: the court often sought to discourage it, especially when they thought the prospective tributary not worth the political price. The imbalance between tribute received and gifts bestowed helped maintain the hierarchical East Asian political order centered on China because it made Chinese vassals understandably eager have their inferior status recognized, thus entitling them to send tribute (Wang, 1998, p. 320). The emperor could even punish vassals by refusing to receive tribute from them – a "punishment" that makes sense only in terms of the disproportionate benefits accruing to the tribute-giver.

Second, the extreme penalties that Ming China prescribed for emigration suggest a country that people were eager to escape, not a country that people were eager to enter. Jiang (2011) puts this down to security concerns (people exiting might betray secrets of China's defense) but the sheer numbers leaving suggest otherwise. Throughout the Ming period Chinese traders, prospectors, and ordinary farmers left the country to settle in Southeast Asia, with tens of thousands later emigrating to Manila and Batavia (Jakarta) in the last century of the dynasty (Lockard, 2013; Willis, 1998, pp. 373–375 and 356–363; Wang, 1959, pp. 10–12). Others settled as far away as Havana, Cuba as Chinatowns emerged throughout Spanish America (Hearn, 2016; Dubs and Smith, 1942). Unlike in China's previous Han golden age, there do not seem to have been major economic migration flows in the opposite direction. Occasionally Chinese who became rich overseas contrived to return to China as foreign ambassadors, but though they were usually spared the death penalty they were rarely allowed to stay (Chan, 1968).

The contrast with the American Tianxia couldn't be clearer. The United States is a magnet for the world's money and talent. People and their money are free to leave the United States at any time, but net flows of both are strongly inward. The Ming *tianxia* promoted the interests of the state (both Chinese and tributary) over the interests of individuals, with the result that individual economic initiative had to be brutally suppressed. The American Tianxia, by contrast, promotes the interests of individuals, certainly over the interests of tributary states and sometimes over the interests of the United States itself. The result is another ironic contradiction: the state that puts the individual first may be more robust than the state that prioritized the state.

Considering that the Ming Dynasty survived for nearly 300 years at the center of the East Asian world-system, this assertion is perhaps still an open question. But entropy theory suggests an answer. Entropy is the ever-present tendency of structures to decay unless energy is injected into the system to keep them up. As every homeowner knows, a house requires constant renovation to fight the ravages of time or it will quickly fall apart. Political systems are subject to the same law. For example, a common interpretation of the decline of the Roman Empire is that the decline became irreversible once Rome stopped expanding; only the continual injection of fresh plunder from the conquest of new territories kept Rome afloat. Ming China was like the late Roman Empire, slowly drawing down its own resources to prevent the decay of its position at the top of the East Asian political hierarchy.

The United States reached its maximum extent more than a century ago. Like Rome, it once thrived on conquest and exploitation. But today the United States fights entropy by continually receiving fresh injections of money and talent from the rest of the world. The American Tianxia is a post-imperial *tianxia*. It doesn't have to conquer external territories to acquire more money and people. The people and money flow in of their own accord.

Hierarchy in the American Tianxia

If the American Tianxia is so different from the Ming *tianxia*, why call it a *tianxia* at all? The American Tianxia may be different in structure from the Ming *tianxia*, but the Ming *tianxia* was only one of many configurations of the East Asian world-system centered on China. In the earliest (Zhou) incarnation of the *tianxia* concept, China itself was not even a united country. In some centuries China was united under native rule, in others united under foreign rule. After the end of the Ming Dynasty in 1644 the tributary system continued (and for a time was strengthened) but the East Asian *tianxia* ceased to be an all-encompassing world-system as it dissolved into the global-scale modern world-system (Zheng and Wu, 2014, p. 59; Babones, 2015d, pp. 10-11; Gordon and Morales Del Pino, 2017). The Ming *tianxia* thus represents the final development of the concept in operation, but not the only form of *tianxia* in history. Analogs of Table 2.1 could be constructed for other periods as well. Only the Confucian ideology would remain a constant. The other structural dimensions would change, depending on the period.

What makes the American Tianxia a *tianxia* is that it encompasses a whole "world" in a central state system based on a universal moral order. Other historical world-systems have not necessarily shared this central state configuration. For example, the Roman Empire was a single political system that effectively subsumed the entire Mediterranean world, but it was a single-state world-empire, not a central state system in which the central state was just one among many states. Medieval Europe, by contrast, was a multi-jurisdictional world-culture tied together by a shared religion that had real political authority. The modern world-system of Wallerstein (1974) and the world-systems school, the world-system that came into existence in the "long" sixteenth century, had no such unifying force, which is why international anarchy is the starting assumption for so much of contemporary international relations theory. None of these historical world-systems operated on the central state model.

The *tianxia* system of pre-modern China and the contemporary world is distinctive in that it is not quite the world-empire of Roman fame nor is it a world-culture on the medieval model. It has repeatedly been characterized as an "American empire," but as Nye (2004, p. 262) says, "while the use of the term may point up some useful analogies, it may also mislead us by obscuring important differences." The parallels between the contemporary world-system and medieval Europe are also strong enough to have sparked discussion of a "new medievalism." The new medievalism in international relations theory describes a non-hierarchical "system of overlapping authority and multiple loyalty" in which states "come to share their authority over their citizens, and their ability to command their loyalties ... with regional and world authorities, and ... with sub-state or sub-national authorities" (Bull, 1977, pp. 245 and 246). It cannot accommodate an overwhelmingly powerful central state that is the origin and arbiter of the universal ideology that claims to govern the citizens of all other states.

The American Tianxia is more like a world-empire on the Roman model than a world-culture on the medieval model. But as a central state system rather than an imperial system it is more akin to the late Roman Republic than to the Roman Empire itself. The difference is that the United States has unwittingly solved the imperial entropy puzzle. Since the early twentieth century the United States has sucked in the resources of the rest of the world without expanding its borders. The position of the United States in the contemporary world-system is thus that of a central state (a *zhongguo*, so to speak) in a hierarchical world-system that is ideologically ordered according to its own fundamental principles (a *tianxia*).

Just as the Chinese word *zhongguo* can only really be applied to China (*Zhongguo*), the word *tianxia* has uniquely East Asian and Confucian connotations in Chinese. But it would be idiomatically ridiculous to refer to the contemporary world-system as an "American all-under-heaven." It makes more sense to bring *tianxia* into English as the proper noun Tianxia. The American Tianxia is thus a hierarchically-ordered world-system of which the United States is the central state and individualism is the dominant ideology.

Like the Chinese *tianxia*, the American Tianxia is roughly divided into five hierarchical levels that reflect proximity to both symbolic and temporal power, as summarized in the bottom half of Table 2.1. The United States itself corresponds to the Ming state in the Confucian five-level hierarchy, with a "royal" (or at least ruling) center that runs along the east coast of the United States from Washington, DC through New York to Boston and subsidiary domains that cover the rest of the United States proper. The northeastern United States hosts an overwhelming concentration of the country's (and the world's) leading governmental, financial, and educational institutions, and its GDP per capita is much higher than that of the rest of the country (Babones, 2017b). The remainder of the United States is a culturally and politically unified zone comparable to the ethnically Chinese component of the Ming empire, clearly part of the central state but not at the center of the center.

In addition to its Han Chinese territories, the Ming empire also encompassed the territories of several "pacified barbarian" peoples who were inside the empire for most purposes but who followed their own customs in civil affairs. They find a contemporary parallel in the four US Anglo-Saxon allies (United Kingdom, Canada, Australia, New Zealand) with which the United States shares an integrated signals intelligence network ("ECHELON") and full military interoperability (Babones, 2015a, p. 59). Interestingly, despite their nominally interior status, the Ming Dynasty did not always support its internal barbarians in their claims against external powers (Jiang, 2011, pp. 100–102), just as the United States does not always support its Anglo-Saxon allies in international disputes. Nonetheless, the elite citizens of these "internal" allies are able to participate in American global governance, enjoying easy mobility among top-level institutions in all five countries. It is no coincidence that of the world's top 10 think tanks, six are located in the United States and three in the United Kingdom (McGann, 2016, p. 49).

Much of the rest of the world, including most of its top economic powers, is broadly aligned with the United States. Khong (2013, p. 22) ranks South Korea, Australia, the United Kingdom, Canada, France, Germany, Italy, Japan, the Netherlands, and Spain as the top 10 "tributary" allies of the United States. Though his ranking method does not include any direct measures of economic size, these happen to be 10 of the 16 largest economies outside the United States (World Bank, 2016). The fourth zone of the American Tianxia, equivalent to Ming China's "tributary barbarians," includes the 25 remaining NATO allies; non-NATO European countries like Austria, Finland, Ireland, Sweden, and Switzerland; Pacific treaty allies like Japan, South Korea, the Philippines, and Thailand; the many US military partners in Africa, the Middle East, and Southeast Asia; many passively aligned countries in Latin America; and increasingly India. None of these countries could be described as anti-systemic in orientation.

Adherence to world society norms of human rights, democracy, and rule of law is an absolute prerequisite for a country's admission to the core of the American Tianxia, with those inside the core of the system vehemently exhorting "barbarian" countries on the outside to accept what are billed as the universal principles of civilized life in the twenty-first century. Some overtly illiberal countries cling to membership in the fourth zone of the American Tianxia due to their strategic location (Turkey, Djibouti) or through command over strategic resources (the Persian Gulf monarchies). Others fall into the fifth zone of unaligned and enemy states. These "wild" barbarian countries are of four types: countries that lack comprehensive state institutions and thus are effectively ungoverned (Afghanistan, Somalia), countries that are ruled by vehemently anti-US regimes (Iran, North Korea), countries that seek recognition of peer-to-peer status in their dealings with the United States (Russia, China), and countries that are in effect client states of Russia and China (Syria, Cambodia). The first two types are irrelevant for understanding the structure of the larger world-system, while the others obviously depend on the positions of China and Russia in that system.

In the 1990s, post-Soviet Russia seemed poised to join the fourth zone of the American Tianxia. Russia was even admitted to the G-7 summit group of economically-advanced democracies, and though it was always more of an aspirational than a real peer of the other seven members it remained a member until Russia's annexation of Crimea in 2014. But Russia's President Vladimir Putin reversed course on Russia's internationalization soon after taking over from Boris Yeltsin in 1999. In his landmark 2007 Munich Security Conference speech he decried the loss of sovereignty implied by participation in a "unipolar" world in which "there is one master, one sovereign" (implicitly, the United States), saying that "the model itself is flawed because at its basis there is and can be no moral foundations for modern civilisation." Since then the Westphalian sovereign equality of states has become the official international relations doctrine of the Russian state.

Sovereign equality is one thing; actual equality quite another. Though Russia is a major military power, its economy is only the thirteenth largest in the world, smaller than Australia's (World Bank, 2016). Its economic and population growth are stagnant, and it faces serious security threats on all of its borders, especially in the east, where it is, ironically, perhaps the country most threatened by the rise of China (Babones, 2015b). Ironically, because on June 25, 2016, Russia and China signed a Declaration on the Promotion of International Law in which they affirm that they "share the view that the principle of sovereign equality is crucial for the stability of international relations." Russia may insist on sovereign equality with the United States in the formulation, interpretation, and (crucially) enforcement of international law, but few people outside Russia take it seriously. China is another matter.

The 1640s all over again

The various social science literatures and the popular press are overflowing with books on the rise of China, and no wonder. Between 1980 and 2015 the Chinese economy grew by a factor of 25, doubling roughly every seven and a half years over a period of 35 years (World Bank, 2016). Real GDP per capita per capita grew by a factor of 20, from around $350 in 1980 to $7000 in 2015. China overtook Japan to become the world's second-largest economy in 2010. China's total GDP is now more than half of the US level. Were it to continue to double every seven or eight years, China would surpass the United States in total GDP by 2025 and even in GDP per capita sometime after mid-century. Such scenarios feed the hopes and fears of many a prognosticator. They form the bedrock foundation for the aggressive (even "hubristic") confidence of the Chinese foreign policy establishment in the imminence of a China-dominated world-system (Lynch, 2015, pp. 155-198). Faith in the emergence of a new Chinese *tianxia* to guide the international affairs not just of East Asia but of the entire world depends on the continued rapid growth of the Chinese economy.

Chinese intellectuals aren't the only ones to pin their hopes on the dynamism of the Chinese economy. In his 2007 Munich speech Vladimir Putin did the same, suggesting the China and India together had already overtaken the United States and that "the economic potential of the new centres of global economic growth will inevitably be converted into political influence and will strengthen multipolarity" – Putin's hope being that a stronger China would not become dominant, but would instead create space for Russia, too, to join some kind of global great power league. Strangely, predictions that China will soon overtake the United States also give cheer to many prominent leftist intellectuals. Both Harvey (2003, p. 200) and Arrighi (2007, pp. 214 and 287) predicted (approvingly) the global dominance of a future Eurasian alliance led by China, vaguely suggesting that this might somehow make the world more democratic. Zizek (2011, pp. 174-176) seems to agree. Leftist intellectual rooting for the rise of

China is very clearly driven by their hope that a powerful China will undermine what they see as American imperialism, though it is not obvious that a Chinese-dominated world would be less imperialist than a US-dominated one.

Like leftist Western intellectuals, the Western international relations establishment has a strong professional interest in the rise of China, since their entire theoretical edifice is built on the analysis of the competitive Westphalian interstate system (Wohlforth, 1999, p. 38). International relations theory thrives on conflict. Even as the conservative columnist Charles Krauthammer (1990) was proclaiming the arrival of a "unipolar" world after the demise of the Soviet challenge, Mearsheimer (1990, p. 56) saw fit to make the spectacularly incorrect prediction that if the Soviet Union were to fully withdraw from Europe "the stability of the past 45 years is not likely to be seen again in the coming decades." Layne (1993, p. 7) mirrored Mearsheimer by characterizing Krauthammer's "unipolar moment" as "just that, a geopolitical interlude that will give way to multipolarity between 2000-2010." Frustrated by the apparent delay in the arrival of challengers to US dominance, Layne (2006, p. 38) later reiterated this prediction with a dilated time frame, to 2030 instead of 2010. Evolving predictions that Germany (Mearsheimer, 1990), Japan (Layne, 1993), the European Union (Layne, 2006), and now China are destined to challenge the United States for global dominance demonstrate the desperation of a discipline that needs such a conflict to justify its own existence.

The return to a multipolarity, so long anticipated, is now almost universally accepted in international relations circles as an imminent, if not already-present, reality (Schweller and Pu, 2011, pp. 41-43; Brooks and Wohlforth, 2016a, pp. 3-5). To find people who are not so convinced that China is rising (or indeed has risen) to the status of a peer challenger of the United States, one must look to China itself, where the economics profession is collectively quite pessimistic about China's ability to surpass the United States (Lynch, 2015, pp. 20-67). Certainly the mass capital flight from China suggests that China's own people are far from confident about the future of the Chinese economy.

Gunter (2017) estimates that capital flight cost China $3.2 trillion between 1984 and 2014, accelerating in later years to a figure of $425 billion for 2014 alone. The Institute of International Finance (2017) estimates that net capital outflows from China rose to $676 billion in 2015 and $725 billion in 2016, with a prediction of over $1 trillion for 2017. To put that $1 trillion figure in context, it is equal to about one-third of China's foreign currency reserves or about one-twelfth of China's GDP. Although the Chinese government continues to maintain that its economy is stably growing at 6.7 percent, this growth is now almost entirely based on deficit spending and forced investment by state-owned enterprises, if it is occurring at all (Babones, 2016).

All good things must come to an end. The trick is to get the time scale right. Predictions of the end of the unipolar interstate system centered on the United States must eventually turn out to be correct, but the American *tianxia* argument suggests that international relations scholars have grossly underestimated the time scale over which its life should be measured. Similarly, China's extraordinary run of economic growth must come to an end. But will it come to an end in 2040, when "China's share of global GDP – 40 percent – will dwarf that of the United States (14 percent) and the European Union (5 percent)," as once predicted by Nobel Prize-winning economist Robert Fogel (2010, p. 70)? Or will it end rather sooner?

Fogel arrived at his outsized predictions for the Chinese economy by forecasting China's economic growth using conventional macroeconomic tools. A slightly less optimistic reading of the same tea leaves has China's economy overtaking the United States in 2032 and remaining only slightly larger than that of the US in 2040 (Dadush and Stancil, 2010). Either way, China seems destined to challenge, if not displace, the United States at the top of the global economic hierarchy. But these economic models analyze the Chinese economy using standard economic inputs like labor, capital, and technology. They do not account for structural factors like politics, culture, behavior, and the environment. Such "soft" factors are difficult to measure directly, but their impacts can be inferred by comparative and historical analogy. Comparative and historical analyses may lack the precision of economic modeling, but they allow for the consideration of a broader range of societal attributes.

A comparative analysis suggests that over the last three decades China has been transformed from a backwards, badly-managed communist society into a typical, state-dominated market economy. The levels and structure of state ownership, corruption, taxation, government spending, education, and healthcare are all similar to those found in other middle income countries like Brazil, Mexico, Russia, and Turkey. These countries started the post-war era with very different economies and societies but through processes of opening and liberalization have all ended up with similar statistical profiles. The main difference is that whereas in the other countries economic elites have captured the government, in China governing elites have captured the economy (Babones, 2012, p. 33). A simple structuralist model of China's convergence with Brazil "suggests that China's extraordinary rate of economic growth will fall back to global norms after 2020" (Babones, 2012, p. 29). It is impossible to know in advance whether or not this prediction will be borne out, but China's growth rate has already fallen well below Fogel's (2010) long-term model prediction of 8 percent. It is still nominally above Dadush and Stancil's (2010) long-term model prediction of 5.6 percent. If the comparative-historical approach is correct, we will know by 2020.

A longer-term historical analysis suggests another structural analogy. Over the course of the Ming Dynasty the Chinese economy was transformed from a non-monetary feudal economy based on mandatory service and customary rents into an export-oriented market economy (Gordon and Morales Del Pino, 2017). The late Ming period from the foundation of Portuguese Macao in 1557 and Spanish Manila in 1571 to the collapse of the dynasty in 1644 saw the transformation of the Chinese economy from a feudal, agrarian economy into a monetized, export-oriented economy that was highly integrated into networks of regional and global trade (Atwell, 1998, pp. 404-406). That transformation of the Chinese economy was facilitated by the import of tens of thousands of tons of monetary silver from central European, Japanese, and (especially) New World sources (Atwell,

1982). In essence, money flowed into China and exports flowed out. Once the Chinese economy reached full monetization, the prices of goods in China (expressed in terms of *taels* of silver, the unit of account in China), especially the price of gold, equalized with prices in the rest of the world (Flynn and Giraldez, 1995). As a result, the trading bonanza came to an end, Chinese exports stabilized, and (perhaps not coincidentally) in 1644 the Ming Dynasty collapsed.

In a striking parallel to the Ming China of the early 1500s, the Communist China of the 1970s had an inward-turned, non-market economy. Both governments sought to avoid trade with the outside world, and when trade was absolutely necessary to route it through official channels. Both governments prohibited emigration and tightly controlled even internal migration. In both cases the arrival of Europeans and Americans (in the 1500s, Latin Americans) was associated with the opening up of the formerly closed system, and in both cases that opening was achieved through the lure of Western money. Then as now the West had little to export to China but money, resulting in the dramatically lopsided net flow of goods out of China. Money poured in and goods poured out until the arbitrage opportunities for simply buying cheap in China and selling dear in the rest of the world began to dry up. Just as in the 1640s, it has now become hard work to make money from trade with China.

Since China's opening in 1979, most economic relationships in China have been transformed from a non-monetary to a monetary basis. People used to be housed, clothed, and fed by their work units; now they work for money, and buy their own. The monetization of all those previously non-monetary arrangements required a vast expansion of the Chinese economy (measured in monetary terms) and sparked enormous increases in productivity that expanded the economy still further. But all that has come to an end. These days everyone in China works for money. If they are retired, they receive their pensions in money. China may still be ruled by a Communist Party, but it is no longer a communist country. No one has estimated the proportion of China's growth of the last three decades that was simply due to the transition from communism to capitalism, but it must be large – and it is over. China's ruling Communist Party can likely withstand falling exports (since 2014), falling foreign currency reserves (since 2014), and rising government budget deficits (since 2011) without collapsing like the Ming Dynasty did. But it can only make the transition to capitalism once. The Party may live on, but the party is over.

3

One belt, one road to nowhere

Boastful predictions (or dire warnings) about the rise of China support an entire intellectual industry of China specialists, authors, and consultants. Indeed, China is an important country that gave rise to one of the world's most prominent civilizations, is a permanent member of the United Nations Security Council, boasts the world's second-largest economy, and is home to nearly 20 percent of the world's population. These superlatives are factually correct, but the language in which they are expressed often seems to tip over from the analytical into the apocalyptic. The most famous example of this is Martin Jacques' (2009) self-explanatory *When China Rules the World*, but similarly extravagant viewpoints can be found in books by such luminaries as Henry Kissinger and Hank Paulson, as well as many other, lesser stars. Callahan (2014, pp. 29-31) suggests that the now-common characterization of China as a unique force shaping the course of human history constitutes a new form of orientalism, though one that associates the mysterious East with hidden reserves of power rather than unfathomable reservoirs of backwardness. It suggests that (Western) economic laws do not apply to China.

Those laws include the limits imposed by political, environmental, and demographic buffers that likely are already retarding China's potential rate of economic growth (Babones, 2011, pp. 84-85). There is also the simple structural fact that that growing from low to middle income status is much easier than growing from middle to high income status. South Korea grew from one-thirtieth to one-third of US levels of GDP per capita between 1960 and 1990 – a growth trajectory even more remarkable than China's (Babones, 2011, p. 81). A quarter century later, it still has not reached half of the US level (World Bank, 2016). Despite 35 years of remarkable growth, China's GDP per capita is still less than one-sixth that of the United States. It may yet reach one-third. But to grow from there to parity – seemingly a minimum requirement to mark "the end of the Western world and the birth of a new global order," as per Jacques' (2009) subtitle – would require yet another wholesale transformation of China. And were such a transformation to occur, one might reasonably ask: would China still be China? A China that changes enough by the middle of the twenty-first century to be more productive and more sophisticated than not just the United States of today but the United States of the middle of the twenty-first century would presumably be a very different China from the age-old civilization of the neo-orientalists.

Before China assumed the mantle of world's next economic superpower, that title was held by Japan. After a quarter century of economic and demographic stagnation, no one talks about Japan in those terms today. But when leading Chinese international relations scholar Yan Xuetong suggested in a 2012 newspaper interview that Japan should accommodate itself to an inevitable future of Chinese dominance, very few Japanese analysts were "willing to accept that Japan is in a state of terminal decline" (Mauch, 2014, p. 202). Japan remains the world's third-largest economy and one of the world's best-equipped military powers (Liff and Ikenberry, 2014, pp. 73–78). Moreover, its military capabilities are almost entirely focused on the threat posed by China (Koga, 2016), whereas for China, Japan is only one of many potential threats. Yan himself believes that a future military confrontation between China and Japan is a "major risk" (Yan, 2014, p. 184). Perhaps more worryingly, Yan considers war with other neighbors to be a possibility as well.

China has had difficult relations with Japan ever since the days of the Ming *tianxia*, when China helped defend Korea against Japanese invasions in 1592 and 1597. But today the United States maintains strong forward positions throughout the old Ming *tianxia*: 28,500 troops in South Korea (Manyin et al., 2016, p. i), 19,000 marines on Okinawa in the Ryuku island chain (Chanlett-Avery and Rinehart, 2016, p. 4), a mutual defense treaty with the Philippines, a pledge to sell arms to Taiwan under the 1979 Taiwan Relations Act, and an increasingly-friendly military relationship with Vietnam (Tow and Limaye, 2016). It's no wonder that Chinese international relations experts are "pessimistic about China's relations with its neighboring states" (Feng and He, 2015, p. 95). As a result of this perceived encirclement by the United States and its allies,

> both the Chinese public and Chinese elites believe the United States is essentially hostile to the most basic Chinese goals ... and that the only long-term solution is for China to gain enough relative strength to reorient the international system so that it is more favorable to Chinese interests. (Roy, 2016, p. 197)

For more than three decades after the beginning of the reform era China single-mindedly pursued this solution. In the wake of 1989's Tiananmen Square massacre, the Chinese leader Deng Xiaoping formalized China's patience game into the famous "24 Character Strategy": "observe calmly; secure our position; cope with affairs calmly; hide our capacities and bide our time; be good at maintaining a low profile; and never claim leadership." In 2009, Deng's protégé Hu Jintao amended the final two points to "firmly uphold keeping a low profile and actively achieve something" (Menon, 2016, p. 132). Yan (2014) understands the Deng-Hu "keeping a low profile" (KLP) strategy as one focused on China's own economic development, contrasting it with Xi Jinping's more militant (though, Yan insists, also more moral) "striving for achievement" (SFA) strategy. With respect to China's neighborhood relations, SFA became official policy in 2013 (Xu, 2016, p. 480). The SFA strategy "clearly refers to economic help to developing countries which leaves no room for misinterpretation" (Yan, 2014, p. 168).

Mutatis mutandis, SFA in operation looks a lot like the early Ming Dynasty tributary system, with contemporary Chinese economic diplomacy taking the place of imperial gift exchange largesse (Pan and Lo, 2017, pp. 9-11). The difference is that the former core tributaries of East Asia are no longer in play. Instead the renewed Chinese tributary system under Xi Jinping consists of the "three planned sub-regional economic communities" of "the silk economic belt in Central Asia, the economic corridor of China, India, Bangladesh, and Myanmar in South Asia, and the maritime silk route in South East Asia" (Yan, 2014, p. 169). Given that China's relationship with India is chronically strained, it seems safe to assume that Yan's second "sub-regional economic community" is likely to remain inoperative for some time. But in late 2013 the new administration of Xi Jinping announced two initiatives that correspond to Yan's first and third communities: the "Silk Road Economic Belt" and the "21st Century Maritime Silk Road." In China's unique language of policy slogans, these two communities together constitute "One Belt, One Road" (1B1R), sometimes also called the "New Silk Road." The 1B1R framework is in effect the masterplan for China's new tributary system.

Eurasian fantasies

Chinese President Xi Jinping announced the first prong of what was to become the 1B1R framework in a September 7, 2013 speech at Nazarbayev University in Kazakhstan. In a speech heavily laden with the rhetoric of Westphalian sovereignty and non-interventionism, Xi proposed the creation of a "Silk Road Economic Belt" that would pursue five priorities: (1) to strengthen policy communication, (2) to improve road connectivity, (3) to promote trade facilitation, (4) to enhance monetary circulation, and (5) to strengthen people-to-people exchanges. The first and last points are clearly platitudinous. The fourth point may sound odd at first reading, but in the full text Xi explains that "the parties should promote the realization of exchange and settlement of local currency." It is a response to the widespread use of the US dollar throughout Central Asia, where dollarization rates "are among the highest in the world" (Ben Naceur et al., 2015, p. 2). China's interest in promoting the use of local currencies stems from its desire to reduce US economic influence in the region.

Xi's second and third points on connectivity and trade are the ones that have captured the world's attention. One might even say: "imagination." After a century of obscurity in the West, with the region secluded and mostly sealed off under Soviet rule, Central Asia reentered the Western consciousness in 1991 and catapulted to the top of the headlines in the aftermath of the September 11, 2001 attacks, which were planned from neighboring Afghanistan. The reemergence of the countries of Central Asia as independent political actors sparked talk of a new "Great Game" for influence in the region, evoking the nineteenth century competition between Russia and British India (Smith, 1996). The five former Soviet republics of Central Asia (Kyrgyzstan, Kazakhstan, Tajikistan, Turkmenistan, and Uzbekistan) are widely perceived to be unstable and vulnerable to outside influence (Weitz, 2006). With a combined population of less than 70 million, they are dwarfed by their larger neighbors, not just China, India, and Russia but even Iran and Turkey. And although with the end of the intervention in Afghanistan the region is of relatively peripheral interest to US policymakers, the United States remains a key actor in the region as well (Rumer et al., 2016).

China, of course, is the biggest giant of all. Writing eight years before China's formulation of 1B1R as an overarching foreign policy framework, Swanstrom (2005, p. 584) presciently warned that China was seeking to dominate both Central Asia and Southeast Asia "in a similar fashion to the American domination over South and Latin America." He likened the operation of China's contemporary economic diplomacy in Central Asia to that of the classical Chinese tributary system. Over the last decade China's economic interests in the region have only increased. China is now by far the region's largest trading partner and in recent years has announced plans for some $100 billion of infrastructure investment in the region (Rumer et al.,

2016, pp. 9-10). The China-led Asian Infrastructure Investment Bank (AIIB) is also expected to invest heavily in Central Asia, though in its first year of operation (2016) it made only one $27.5 million loan in the region, for improving a border crossing between Tajikistan and Uzbekistan (Hsu, 2017).

China's overwhelming economic presence has brought benefits to Central Asia but also stoked fears. Many sources share a perhaps apocryphal saying from contemporary Kazakhstan: "If you want to leave the country, learn English; if you want to stay, learn Chinese." Clarke (2014, pp. 155-163) uses it to headline a section in which he outlines popular Kazakh fears of Chinese economic exploitation, immigration, and water theft. If such fears are rampant in Kazakhstan they might well be expected to exist in the other four countries as well. Peyrouse (2016) describes a region rife with Sinophobia, tempered only by large-scale elite corruption through which political leaders and their families benefit handsomely from their relationships with Chinese state-owned firms. Close relations with China may be valued an "insurance policy" against Russian domination (Clarke 2014, p. 167), but they are still viewed as "rather dangerous in the long term" (Peyrouse, 2016, p. 23). Chinese money may be popular in the region, but China seemingly is not.

Within China itself, the Silk Road Economic Belt is often portrayed as an extension of China's domestic "Go West" development strategy (Zhang, 2015b, pp. 8-10; Ferdinand, 2016, pp. 951-953). This strategy, formally the "Western Development Program," was launched by President Jiang Zemin in 1999 with the goal of fulfilling Deng Xiaoping's 1992 goal of "overcoming regional inequality by the turn of the century" (Lai, 2002, p. 436). In its early years, funding for the Go West campaign was "distinctly limited," consisting mainly of a rebadging of funds already allocated "before the campaign was publicly articulated" (Goodman, 2004, p. 319). The hope was apparently that private and foreign investment would fill the gap. When these hopes were not fulfilled, the Chinese government began to promote links to Central Asia and beyond in terms of the regional development of the western provinces of China. For example, Xi'an (the symbolic gateway to northwest China) and Chongqing (the symbolic gateway to southwest China) have been made the nominal starting points of new rail freight services through Central Asia to Europe.

In theory, the relatively poor, underdeveloped provinces of western China could benefit from better infrastructure and higher levels of economic development in Central Asia. In practice, the five countries of Central Asia are economically irrelevant for China. The combined $301 billion GDP of Kyrgyzstan, Kazakhstan, Tajikistan, Turkmenistan, and Uzbekistan is 15 percent less than the GDP of central China's relatively poor Anhui province (World Bank, 2016; National Bureau of Statistics, 2016). The economies of Central Asia are simply too small for their development to have any meaningful impact on growth in China. China's economic support for these countries can only be rationalized in terms of Yan's (2014) SFA strategy of economic assistance in exchange for political recognition. Swanstrom certainly views it this way:

> China's intention is ... to influence and control the Central Asian region to a length that could be compared to a classical vassal relationship ... where Beijing invests and provides security and receives political stability and influence in the region. [...] The Chinese strategy is ... to influence the states to the degree that they would, voluntarily or by necessity, view China as the main actor in the region once more. (Swanstrom, 2005, p. 584)

This investment-for-recognition bargain can be seen even more clearly in the extension of the Silk Road Economic Belt to eastern and even western Europe. Europe is too far away to be considered a neighboring region to China, and European Union countries are too rich to require Chinese economic assistance. But that doesn't prevent European countries from accepting Chinese subsidies, when offered. China has signed "comprehensive strategic partnership" agreements with virtually every country in Europe, plus the EU itself. Much trumpeted by Chinese state media, it is not clear what these agreements actually signify (Feng and Huang, 2014). It is clear, however, that any subsidies resulting from these partnerships will flow in one direction: from China to Europe. Chinese state-owned enterprises have made politically-sensitive investments all across Europe. As in Central Asia, these deals have generated unease among some pundits and politicians. But European governments have proven willing to exchange vague assurances of political recognition for immediate Chinese cash subsidies.

The levels of Chinese subsidies embedded in long-term European infrastructure agreements are difficult to quantify, but the subsidies embedded in transportation operations are slightly more transparent. Industry experts estimate that Chinese governments (national and regional) subsidize around half of the cost of shipping containers to Europe (Farchy, 2016), and this doesn't include the losses incurred on empty return trains to China. Though strongly promoted by Xi's 1B1R strategy, China to Europe rail links simply aren't practical for most commodities. The symbolic Yiwu to London rail link, launched January 1, 2017, illustrates the difficulties involved. Four different trains are required to complete the trip, since China and Europe operate on standard gage, the former Soviet republics operate on wide gage, and the Channel Tunnel has distinct technical requirements of its own. Even with massive, politically-motivated subsidies, intercontinental rail lines can carry only a tiny fraction of the volume of freight moved by sea. Since there is no economic rationale for these links, they are likely to disappear the moment the subsidies are withdrawn. It is telling that no European or Central Asian country (not even Russia) has proven willing to join China in investing in the development of trans-Eurasian rail freight.

Last century the British geographer Halford Mackinder (1904, p. 434) predicted that "the century will not be old before all Asia is covered with rail ways" connecting Europe to China and the Pacific. He characterized Central Asia as "the pivot region of the world's politics" that was "about to be covered with a network of railways." He even suggested that China ("organized by the Japanese") might one day conquer Russia and through its control of the pivot region of Central Asia come to dominate the world (p. 437). Mackinder is perennially popular among strategic thinkers, but his century came and went, leaving Central Asia no closer to becoming the "heartland" of the "world-island" of Eurasia (Mackinder, 1919). No amount of Chinese economic assistance will transform Central Asia into the new hub of the global economy, and the whole idea of China (2015 GDP per capita around $8000) subsidizing the European Union (2015 GDP per capita around $32,000) can only be characterized as a bit odd. No doubt European and Central Asian countries will continue to kowtow as long as the subsidies keep flowing. But it is difficult to see how the Silk Road Economic Belt can transform China's geopolitical position over the medium to long term.

The road to nowhere

The second prong of the 1B1R framework was unveiled a month after the first. In an October 2, 2013 speech to the Indonesian Parliament, Chinese President Xi Jinping pledged to work with the countries of the Association of Southeast Asian Nations (ASEAN) to build a "21st Century Maritime Silk Road." It was in this context that he first proposed the creation of the AIIB and suggested that it would "give priority to ASEAN countries' needs," though in fact in its first year of operation the AIIB only made two loans among the 10 ASEAN members, and only one of them was for infrastructure (a power plant in Myanmar) (Hsu, 2017). Most of the AIIB's inaugural funding has gone toward projects in Pakistan and the Middle East. This is perhaps not surprising, given China's myriad maritime disputes with its Southeast Asian neighbors in the South China Sea (Heydarian, 2015). Cambodia is the only Southeast Asian country that has unambiguously friendly relations with China, and even there local politics threaten the stability of that friendship (Hutt, 2016).

Since 2013, China's Maritime Silk Road rhetoric has been extended to cover the Middle East and even Africa, bringing nearly all of Afro-Eurasia under the 1B1R umbrella. Given the presence of multiple strong regional powers in South Asia and the Middle East, Africa has become a particular focus for the Maritime Silk Road. Chinese economic diplomacy does not offer sufficient rewards to sway the foreign policies of countries like India, Iran, and Saudi Arabia, but modest sums can have a substantial impact in some African countries. Moreover, high levels of corruption in Africa tend to facilitate instant access. Since 2004 China has become by far the largest trading partner and one of the largest sources of investment and aid for African countries (Busse et al., 2016, pp. 233-235). Whether or not it does Africa any good is an open question. Busse et al. (2016, pp. 254 and 255) conclude that Chinese aid and investment "seem to play no major role for African countries' economic development," though Chinese imports may "have a negative impact on economic growth."

Though China's 1B1R rhetoric stresses international cooperation and even Chinese generosity in its dealings with less-developed countries, Chinese state support is thoroughly realist in application. Bond (2010, p. 18) suggests that "China's role has been even more predatory than that of Western corporations, backed by its support of local dictators." Chinese foreign direct investment in poor countries is driven almost entirely by state-owned firms, with the result that investment and aid are inextricably linked. Chinese aid to Africa is overwhelmingly focused on those countries that are important sources of raw materials for Chinese state-owned enterprises, especially oil: the top five African recipients of Chinese aid are Angola, Sudan, Ghana, Ethiopia, and Nigeria (Constantaras, 2016). All of these except Ethiopia are major oil exporters. Chinese aid to and investment in Ethiopia are very different from that in the rest of the continent; China seems to be developing Ethiopia as a kind of bridgehead and focal point for its engagement with Africa as a whole (Hackenesch, 2013, pp. 21-25; Hess and Aidoo, 2015, pp. 87-90). In 2011 China even donated a new permanent headquarters building for the African Union in Ethiopia's capital, Addis Ababa.

Other than as a source of oil, Africa's strategic relevance for China's foreign policy is low (Sun, 2014a, p. 30). Yet African countries receive more than 50 percent of China's total foreign aid (Sun, 2014b). Perhaps not coincidentally, Africa is the region that Chinese international relations specialists overwhelmingly perceive to be friendliest toward

China (Feng and He, 2015, pp. 95-96). By contrast, the two countries that they believe are most likely to be involved in a military conflict with China are its two Maritime Silk Road neighbors, the Philippines and Vietnam, which even outpoll Japan (Feng and He, 2015, pp. 95-96). The survey on which these figures are based was conducted in 2012, well before the 2016 election of the China-friendly Rodrigo Duterte as President of the Philippines – but also well before the 2016 United Nations Convention on the Law of the Sea (UNCLOS) ruling in favor of the Philippines that denied Chinese sovereignty claims in the South China Sea. Whatever the personalities of the leaders of the day, the structural realities of China's relationships with most of its Southeast and South Asian neighbors make genuine cooperation difficult.

At the height of its power and prestige in the early fifteenth century, Ming China sought to expand its tributary system throughout the length of what is now called the Maritime Silk Road. The Yongle Emperor (r. 1402-1424), third emperor of the dynasty and son of the founding Hongwu Emperor, ignored his father's advice that the dynasty should leave its southern neighbors in peace and instead focus its energies closer to home (Wang, 1998, p. 319). He commissioned the famous voyages of Zheng He, the seven enormous "treasure fleets" that sailed throughout Southeast Asia and into the Indian Ocean collecting "tribute" from as far away as Somalia. Zheng He's fleets were heavily armed (on the order of the Spanish Armada) and practiced a form of what we might now call "gunboat diplomacy" (Wade, 2005, pp. 51-52), though Wang (1959, p. 7) prefers the term "state trading." All sources agree that the Zheng He treasure fleets were not remunerative; they were prompted by the emperor's "desire for universal legitimation," primarily in support of his political position at home (Wang, 1998, p. 320). In other words, they were a form of economic diplomacy, though perhaps more transparently coercive than their twenty-first century equivalent.

China's current expansionism in the "southern oceans" of the Maritime Silk Road doesn't involve heavily-armed fleets, but it is noteworthy that the most enthusiastic supporters of the Maritime Silk Road are those countries that are safely out of reach of China's growing military power. Like the Ming Dynasty's treasure fleets, the 21st Century Maritime Silk Road will buttress Chinese legitimacy only so long as China continues to offer financial incentives and governments in the region are willing to take them. As a result, China's new 1B1R *tianxia* in Afro-Eurasia is vulnerable to both economic and political instability. Because it (self-consciously) rests on the mutual self-interest of the states involved, it is likely to last only as long as that mutual self-interest persists. This is very different from the structure of the American Tianxia. True, the United States has self-interested allies all across Afro-Eurasia. But neither the convergence of interests nor the much-trumpeted convergence of values is the ultimate basis of US power.

The strength of the American Tianxia is that it is based on individual interests, not national interests. Even in countries that are broadly hostile to US policies, individuals benefit from access to the distinction hierarchies of the American Tianxia. That is true for individuals, especially elite individuals, across all of the 1B1R countries, as well as within China itself.

The American within

The difficulties China has faced in recruiting the peoples of Afro-Eurasia to the Chinese cause are mirrored with greater urgency within China itself. If, as Zhao (2015) argues, the ultimate purpose of China's economic diplomacy is to bolster the legitimacy of the Chinese government in the eyes of the Chinese people themselves, the government's failure to persuade its own population that China is globally respected and admired may be more of a problem than wasteful spending associated with the government's many external initiatives. If China can convince its own elites that the country is on track to be the future center of a renewed Chinese *tianxia* over Afro-Eurasia, they may be persuaded to invest in Xi Jinping's "China Dream" of "a rich and powerful country, revitalizing the nation and enhancing the well-being of the people" (Ferdinand, 2016, p. 946). If China cannot win over its elites, they have the ability to move themselves and their money to other jurisdictions. Capital flight is one indicator of a lack of confidence, but capital flight may also indicate the legitimate desire to diversify holdings, or even just an undervalued currency. Emigration is different: expensive and traumatic. It reflects a serious, multigenerational commitment to identity change.

China's emigration rates are low but disproportionately skewed toward the wealthy, skilled, and educated (Xiang, 2016, p. 3). The United States admits roughly 70,000 Chinese immigrants per year to permanent residence, a level that has been relatively stable throughout the decade (DHS, 2016, Table 10; see also earlier years). The other four Anglo-Saxon countries combined admit a similar number. Thus the net number of Chinese citizens migrating permanently to the core countries of the American Tianxia probably totals somewhere between 100,000 and 150,000 per year, allowing for return migration and repeat temporary migrants who are in effect permanent. But these figures suffer from two serious shortcomings. First, they comingle family reunification and other non-economic flows with true economic migration. Second (and more importantly), they exclude one major long-term flow of permanent economic migration: birth tourism.

All of the Anglo-Saxon countries share a long-standing tradition of the *jus soli* granting of citizenship to nearly all people born on their soil. In the 1980s and 1990s, Australia, New Zealand, and the United Kingdom restricted this right mainly to children of citizens and permanent residents. The United States and Canada, however, continue to grant citizenship on a *jus soli* basis with only minor exceptions. This has given rise to a massive birth tourism industry concentrated in southern California but extending up the west coast of North America to San Francisco, Seattle, and Vancouver.

The Chinese birth tourism industry is especially large in the United States. The origin of this tendency may be the high prestige or perceived benefits associated with US citizenship, but the driving force behind what are widely reported to be rapidly rising numbers is undoubtedly the fact that in November 2014 the US and China signed a reciprocal 10-year multiple entry visa agreement. Previously, Chinese expectant mothers had to rush to acquire visas in the short window between the confirmation of their pregnancies and the point at which they became visibly pregnant, because visa interviews were required for every visit to the United States and pregnant women are widely understood to have been routinely denied visas. Now Chinese women can obtain 10-year multiple entry tourist visas in their early twenties, wait for marriage and pregnancy, then make hassle-free trips to the United States just to give birth. This dramatically lowers the bar for obtaining US citizenship for their babies.

Birth tourism is thus presumably becoming the main avenue for citizenship mobility for Chinese families. "Presumably," because there are no hard data on the size of birth tourism flows. Anecdotal evidence suggests that the number of Chinese women traveling to the United States explicitly for the purpose of acquiring US citizenship for their children has risen rapidly from less than 10,000 per year before 2014 to anywhere from 60-80,000 or more today (Sheehan, 2015). Since young Chinese women granted (renewable) 10-year US multiple entry visas in the first years of the program may have as much as 25 years of fertility ahead of them, the full effects of the changed visa regime may not be realized until the 2020s. In the absence of a centralized US citizenship registry, it will be difficult for researchers to estimate the size these flows, since they do not, technically speaking, constitute immigration. Nonetheless, in the mid-2030s there will be Chinese students at US universities who do not have to return home to China after graduation because they will already be US citizens.

The birth tourism stream is set to become the main channel through which elite Chinese families upgrade their positions within the US-centered American Tianxia. Table 3.1 reports estimates of the sizes of the three major economic migration streams from China to the five Anglo-Saxon countries at the core of the American Tianxia: birth tourism, investor visas, and skilled migration. Birth tourism is only relevant for Canada and the United States; given that no official data are available for this stream, its size has been estimated based on news reports, which are themselves entirely based on anecdotal evidence. For example, the 60,000 figure for 2015 (rising to 80,000 in 2016), reported in Sheehan (2015) and many other sources, is taken from a

Chinese birth tourism trade association brochure. Given the hearsay, self-referencing nature of such "data" there is no point citing sources for the birth tourism estimates in Table 3.1. Suffice it to say they represent best guesses based on available opinion. Data for the other two streams are drawn from official government sources. Approximate ranges are given where the data are ambiguous or highly volatile year-on-year.

Table 3.1: Indicative numbers of Chinese families anchoring in Anglo-Saxon countries annually

Stream	AUS	CAN	NZ	UK	USA
Birth tourism	N/A	1000	N/A	N/A	10–80k
Investor visa	Minor	2k	Minor	Minor	9k
Skilled migration	17k	10k–15k	2k	5k–10k	20k
Indicative total	20k	15k	2k	8k	75k

Birth tourism has the potential to "anchor" a family in the United States (or Canada) by gaining non-Chinese citizenship for one member of the family. Given China's extraordinarily low fertility rate, in many cases this one anchor baby may represent the entire inheritance of two parents and four grandparents. Investor and skills migration are older, better-established streams for achieving the same kind of foreign anchor. Investor visa holders are able to sponsor family members to work in their businesses via the skilled migrant stream, while the children of permanent resident skilled migrants are eligible for citizenship in all five Anglo-Saxon countries.

All of these streams will ultimately result in the migration of many more people from China than the number of anchors, but from a political-economic standpoint it is the number of anchors that counts. The total number of family anchors created across all five countries and all three streams in any given year in the mid-2010s is likely around 120,000. If each of these anchors represents the accumulated family wealth of several post-reform generations, the total transfer of ownership in the Chinese economy from Chinese citizens to US citizens implied by the migration of the owners of that wealth may rival current levels of capital flight from China. At $1 million per family, owner migration represents a notional transfer of $120 billion a year. At $10 million per family, the notional amount rises to $1.2 trillion.

Levels of economic migration from China have been slowly rising throughout the 2010s, but the composition by stream and country is rapidly changing. Skilled migration is relatively stable at around 70,000 per year across all five countries, while the number of investor visas has dropped precipitously as Australia, Canada, New Zealand, and the United Kingdom have severely restricted their programs. The US investor visa program is limited to 10,000 per year (for all nationalities) on a first-come, first-served basis that has resulted in an eight-year waiting list.

With the other two streams stable or declining, the future of economic migration from China lies in birth tourism, and the unambiguous top destination for birth tourism is the United States. There is no firm upper limit to the number of Chinese who may choose to give birth to US citizens. The main barriers are financial: in addition to the one-time cost of giving birth in the US, US citizen children must be educated in private international schools in China. These costs may limit the total numbers, but they also ensure the "quality," so to speak. The fact that Chinese birth tourism is dominated by elites reduces the likelihood of a political backlash in the United States. It also means that the sum total of wealth transfer involved may be staggeringly large.

There is perhaps one recent historical parallel for the family-financial exodus from China to the United States: the post-Soviet influx of Russians into London. In the quarter century since the dissolution of the Soviet Union, London has been transformed by such an avalanche of Russian wealth that people jokingly refer to it as "Londongrad" or "Moscow-on-Thames" (Hopkin and Blyth, 2014). China's population and wealth are literally a magnitude larger than Russia's. If China's post-communist elites fall out with the Chinese government on the same scale as Russia's did, it would be no quirky historical avalanche. It would be an enormous slow-motion political-economic tidal wave of epochal proportions.

Of course, the strange thing about tidal waves is that they are barely perceptible until they reach shore. This one may already be in motion, wide and deep but mostly below the surface. If and when it finally breaks, Calichina will make Londongrad look like a day at the beach. The real new silk road, the one that people really want to travel and the one where the really big money is being made, is the one that ends in Silicon Valley. Eurasia is no longer the "heartland" of the global economy, if it ever was. The crossroads of the twenty-first century digital economy is likely to be in Calichina, if it is anywhere at all.

4

The hiatus of history

It is often said that the twentieth century was the American century. The great popularizer of this idea was Henry Luce, who as publisher of *Life* magazine urged the people of the United States to fulfill what he saw as their historic destiny "to rise to the opportunities of leadership in the world" by joining the fight against Hitler (Luce, 1941, p. 63). In Luce's telling, the American century didn't start at the end of World War II; as Nye (2017, pp. 11–12) reminds us, conventional accounts of American post-war dominance are vastly overblown. No, for Henry Luce, as for Charles Beard (1922) and for Bertrand and Dora Russell (1923), the American century had begun at the start of the twentieth century, not in its middle. Luce said that in 1919, at the end of World War I, the United States had missed "a golden opportunity, an opportunity unprecedented in all history, to assume the leadership of the world – a golden opportunity handed to us on a proverbial silver platter" (Luce, 1941, p. 64).

Luce is well-remembered for calling the twentieth century the American century, but he is not well-remembered for calling the twentieth century the "first" American century (Luce, 1941, pp. 64 and 65). Luce strongly implied that it would not be the last. Though declinism is a recurring theme among members of the US international relations establishment, there are some who share Luce's point of view.

Nye (2015) addresses Luce quite directly in the title of his book: *Is the American Century Over?* His answer is unambiguously no. Taking into account a multitude of economic, political, military, and cultural aspects of global leadership, he concludes that "the American century is not over ... we have not entered a post-American world" (Nye, 2015, p. 125). Wohlforth (1999, p. 37) presciently came to this conclusion two decades earlier, recognizing that "unipolarity is not a 'moment.' It is a deeply embedded material condition of world politics that has the potential to last for many decades."

Wohlforth (1999, p. 39) calls this new unipolar era the "Pax Americana," while emphasizing that it is much more global and much more a peace than the nineteenth century Pax Britannica ever was. And peace it is, at least from an international perspective. Most of the highly-visible, distressingly-violent conflicts going on around the world today are not international wars fought with the objective of gaining territory. They are civil wars, or interventions in civil wars, or interventions to change governments. Yet Wohlforth gives the Pax Americana only "many decades" of potential future life. Why not "many centuries"? After all, the Roman original lasted at least two centuries, and if civil wars are ignored, perhaps as long as five centuries. The Ming *tianxia* lasted nearly 300 years, and the succeeding Qing Dynasty (1644-1911) tributary system operated smoothly for another 200 years before European encroachments led to its destabilization. Why should the American Tianxia be any different?

At issue here is what Chase-Dunn (1998, pp. 321-322) calls the "width of a time point." Finding the appropriate width of a time point is crucial for meaningful forecasting. Most social scientists are loath to make predictions, whether out of epistemological commitment or out of a simple fear of being proved wrong. But social science forecasting is entirely feasible, given an appropriate time horizon. For example, it is certain that in the 2020s China and India will be the two countries with the largest populations in the world, with India overtaking China in or around that decade (UNPD, 2015). Population forecasting is feasible over a time scale of half a century or more because even though population statistics are reported as annual figures, the relevant width of a time point for population is much larger. The United States only conducts a full census once every 10 years because finer-grained population figures really aren't that useful. The decade is a sufficient time unit for understanding population.

Political systems change even more slowly than population. The Westphalian interstate system lasted from the 1640s until the 1940s, at which point it broke down under the pressure of a new reality: the rise of the United States to global dominance. As Luce, Beard, Russell, and many others realized at the time, the United States was already dominant in the first half of the twentieth century; it simply chose not to operationalize that dominance in the sphere of international relations. Luce (1941, p. 65) cited the global dominance of "American jazz, Hollywood movies, American slang, American machines and patented products"; he claimed that the United States was "already the intellectual, scientific and artistic capital of the world." He also strongly implied that the US held the world's purse strings; the US has had the world's largest economy since the late nineteenth century. Even today, China is only an economic peer of the United States if adjustments are made for purchasing power parity, and that with a population more than four times the size.

Implicitly recognizing the "width of a time point" problem, Brooks and Wohlforth (2016b, p. 33) contend that "the gap between economic parity and a credible bid for superpower status should be measured over many decades." But even so their model assumes that China will soon reach economic parity with the United States. They are skeptical of China's technological capacity for global leadership, but they underestimate "the longevity of today's one-superpower system" (p. 53) because they follow consensus opinion in taking for granted China's economic convergence with the United States. Forecasts of future Chinese economic power routinely assume that China will simultaneously continue to grow in per capita terms while remaining a country that is four times the population of the United States. The economy is one thing; demographics are quite another. Whether or not China continues to get richer, it will certainly get smaller – much smaller.

Mechanistically wishful thinking about the future of the Chinese economy is nothing new. Already in 2001, Yan Xuetong presented a charmingly straightforward theory of China's looming global dominance:

> The Chinese Government plans to make China a developed country by 2050. If the Chinese standard of living catches up with that of the European Union (EU), China's economic size will be 3.2 times that of the EU's GDP because China has a population 3.2 times larger. [...] An economy 3.2 times that of the EU means one that is 1.4 times larger than the total GDP of the EU, the United States, and Japan combined. (Yan, 2001, p. 38)

Such rosy scenarios ignore China's one-child reality. Based on inputs from official data, China's population will peak in 2026 at just over 1.4 billion, after which will start falling rapidly (Census Bureau, 2017). Thus by 2050 China is projected to have a population of 1.3 billion, compared to 400 million for the United States and nearly 550 million for the Anglo-Saxon core of the American Tianxia. But these figures are based on three problematic assumptions: first, that China's official fertility rate of 1.7 children per woman is in fact the true figure; second, that China will maintain a fertility rate of 1.6 for the next four decades; and third, that China's sex ratio at birth will rapidly fall from today's morbid 110 boys per 100 girls (Huang et al., 2016) to a more normal 106 (for most Western countries the figure is 105). Of these three assumptions, the first is almost certainly wrong, the second is dubious, and the third impossible to predict.

The US Census Bureau, the United Nations Population Division, and other official bodies base their projections on China's official statistics. With life expectancy slowly increasing and negligible net migration, the main unknown in the 2050 population projection of 1.3 billion for China is the fertility rate. Chinese official data report a total fertility rate of 1.7, and the US Census Bureau duly uses a slightly modified assumption of 1.6 in its models. But the Chinese

Academy of Social Sciences put the rate at 1.4 in a report that received sufficient political backing to have been covered by China's official state broadcaster (CGTN, 2015). Calculations based on China's own official births data suggest the real figure in 2014 may have been 1.2, perhaps falling to as low as 1.05 in 2015 (Babones, 2015c; Huang, 2016). These figures may incorporate slight downward biases due to non-registration of second births, but any such impact would be slight (Huang et al., 2016).

If China's true fertility rate is around 1.2, not 1.6 as assumed by the Census Bureau, then current and future birth cohorts will be some 25 percent smaller than modeled. If Chinese parents continue to select for male offspring, low fertility will be exacerbated by smaller cohorts of women. Extrapolating these fertility trends out to 2100 suggests a century's end population for China of less than 600 million (People's Daily, 2016). Such an extrapolation is not unrealistic: all of China's richer East Asian neighbors have similarly low fertility rates (Raymo et al., 2015). The five Anglo-Saxon countries, with replacement-level fertility rates and consistent in-migration would be projected to grow to roughly the same population level as China. Crossing these two trends produces a remarkable scenario: that China's population in 2100 might be roughly the same as (or even less than) that of the Anglo-Saxon core of the American Tianxia.

There are too many uncertainties involved for demographic predictions on such a long time scale to be taken at face value, but the exercise is suggestive. If it is inappropriate to definitely conclude that the Anglo-Saxon countries will overtake China in population by 2100, it is equally inappropriate to assume that China will retain its massive demographic advantage. Considering the long-established trend of migration toward all of the Anglo-Saxon countries and the low fertility rates of all of the East Asian countries, the balance of plausibility seems to strongly favor the demographic parity scenario, if not by 2100 then soon afterward. Assuming that China does not catch up with the United States in GDP per capita – a feat that has so far eluded both South Korea (49 percent) and Japan (58 percent) – it will recede as a conceivable global challenger by mid-century.

By the middle of the twenty-first century it is likely that China's economy will be smaller (relative to that of the United States) than it is today, and by the end of the century China's relative shrinkage is almost certain. Moreover, as Starrs (2013) documents, much of the Chinese economy isn't Chinese at all. This is especially true of its technologically leading sectors, many of which are embedded in global value chains that are dominated by US companies (Brooks and Wohlforth, 2016a, pp. 38-44). Other relevant factors play out on an even longer time scale than demographics. For example, a structural feature of China's geography is that, unlike the United States, China is surrounded by large, wary, and potentially hostile neighbors (Chen and Pan, 2011, pp. 80-82). Simply put, it is hard to find a path through which China becomes a peer competitor to the United States – and it is even harder to find any other potential competitor.

But if the American Tianxia thesis is correct, competition is beside the point. Everyone who is employed in a global value chain, pursues a university degree, or enters the US Green Card lottery is part of the American Tianxia. Migrants to Europe from Africa and the Middle East who believe that a European education will gain their children entry into elite global labor markets are also part of the American Tianxia. China's growing numbers of US babies are definitely destined for membership in the American Tianxia, whether or not they ultimately move to the United States, and with up to 100,000 Chinese babies being born US citizens every year, birth tourism may result in millions of new elite Chinese-Americans. The twenty-first century may indeed turn out to be the Chinese century, but if so it will not be China's century. It will be the century of the Chinese people overseas, whether in Singapore, Taiwan, Canada, or, increasingly, the United States. Calichina may one day emerge as the most important center of the American Tianxia.

The American Tianxia as social fact

The great philosopher of the state Georg Hegel maintained that "the History of the World is nothing but the development of the Idea of

Freedom" (Hegel, 1861, p. 476). Francis Fukuyama famously found that freedom at the "end of history" in 1989. Some three decades on, it is worth remembering that Fukuyama called the end of history before the Tiananmen Square massacre, before the fall of the Berlin Wall, and well before the dissolution of the Soviet Union. Even so, Fukuyama recognized that:

> What we may be witnessing is not just the end of the Cold War, or the passing of a particular period of postwar history, but the end of history as such: that is, the end point of mankind's ideological evolution and the universalization of Western liberal democracy as the final form of human government. (Fukuyama, 1989, p. 4)

Seemingly appalled by the intellectual world's embrace and condemnation alike, Fukuyama soon began rolling back the end of history thesis, claiming that his argument was merely normative (not empirical) (Fukuyama, 1995). He questions whether or not "liberal democracy is a good thing," concluding, "provisionally, that liberal democracy satisfies the different parts of the soul more completely than its competitors, but one has to know whether the soul exists, and if so, of what it consists" (p. 43). On this he proclaims that "it is impossible to be anything but pessimistic" (p. 43).

This is a long way from his earlier, pragmatic assertion that "large-scale conflict must involve large states still caught in the grip of history, and they are what appear to be passing from the scene" (Fukuyama, 1989, p. 18). Fukuyama did confess himself "sad" in 1989, but sad along with Friedrich Nietzsche and Leo Strauss that there would be no more great causes for great men to fight for. Not for nothing did Fukuyama (1992) expand his title to *The End of History and the Last Man* – the "last man" being Nietzsche's derogatory term for the comfortable, satisfied, well-fed antithesis of the superman. Fukuyama's pessimism is not pessimism for the prospects of liberal democracy. It is pessimism for life itself.

In both his 1989 essay and his 1992 book, Fukuyama identifies Hegel's end of history with the "universal homogeneous [or homogenous] state." This he defines "as liberal democracy in the political sphere combined with easy access to VCRs and stereos in the economic" (Fukuyama, 1989, p. 8). Leaving aside Fukuyama's obvious shortcomings as a futurologist, does this formula capture the contemporary zeitgeist? Liberalism, yes, and consumer goods, certainly. But democracy? If liberal democracy is the end of history, then the democratic nation-state is the end of history, because only nation-states (or entities approximating them) have ever been known to be democratic. This is the argument behind the Russian state doctrine of "sovereign democracy." But other than through force of habit, why assume that democracy is a defining characteristic of the universal homogeneous state at the end of history?

Democracy may have been more popular in 1989 than it is now. Today many liberal internationalists decry populism, most condemn the Brexit referendum outcome, and nearly all decry the Presidency of Donald Trump. Democracy is not always liberal. Many people believe that democracy is a good thing, and for good reasons. But is it really part of the end of history?

Fukuyama's concept of the universal homogeneous state is derived, not directly from Hegel, but from Hegel's great twentieth century interpreter, Alexander Kojeve. Kojeve (1969, p. 95) clarifies that by the universal state he means one that is "nonexpandable" and by the homogeneous state he means one that is "non-transformable" in the dialectical sense, or in simpler terms (p. 90) "free from internal contradictions: from class strife, and so on." Nowhere did Kojeve mention democracy. In fact, his model of the universal and homogeneous state was Napoleon's empire (Kojeve, 1969, p. 69). Contrary to perceptions that he is an American jingoist, Fukuyama's model of the universal and homogeneous state is the only slightly more democratic European Union (Fukuyama, 2007). And everyone agrees that Hegel himself was certainly no democrat.

Leaving aside democracy, the conundrum for the universal homogeneous state is how to be universal within a single nation-state. The Ming *tianxia* and the American Tianxia are both universal in their own terms, but not nation-states. The American Tianxia is near-universal in any terms. It is also homogeneous, at least in the limited sense in which Kojeve used the term. The American Tianxia encompasses vast inequalities, but a defining feature of US political life has always been a lack of strong class identification. Classlessness is even more a feature of the American Tianxia, for although there are massive inequalities in today's world they are not primarily aligned on a class axis. They are driven by myriad individual factors (citizenship, industry, talent, schooling, etc.), and their individuality is the antithesis of class. There are 7 billion "internal contradictions" or none; at least, there are none that are likely to lead to the transformation of the system, because there is no Hegelian master–slave dialectic in the American Tianxia.

The American Tianxia is the universal homogeneous state that Fukuyama was looking for but did not quite find at the end of history. Its defining ideology of liberalism is more expansive, more universal, and (one might say) more attractive than the Ming Dynasty's state Confucianism. Whereas Ming China exported governing ideas, the United States exports governing ideals. The American Tianxia is not quite a state, but it has attributes of a state, and is a kind of global state-within-the-state, as well as a state-within-the-mind. It would be impossible to have a central state system like the American Tianxia without a central state, but the system itself is much larger than the central state. Wherever people seek success in global distinction hierarchies, or even seek the prestige that high status in global distinction hierarchies gives them in local hierarchies, they voluntarily place themselves under the administration of the American Tianxia. Most people have no democratic say in how online social networks are managed, how MBA degrees are awarded, or how multinational firms conduct their hiring. They seek distinction in such arenas regardless.

Democracy within countries is clearly a prerequisite for admission to the core of the American Tianxia, but democracy at a global level is not at all a feature – or even an ideal – of the American Tianxia itself. Individuals are the constituent members of the American Tianxia, and individuals have human rights, not democracy. The right to select their local (i.e., national) leaders in democratic elections is one of the many rights accorded to individuals in the American Tianxia, and states can thus be vilified for not respecting this right. Non-democratic states are relegated to the "outer barbarian" levels of the American Tianxia, but their citizens are not. Chinese individuals can be fully accepted into the distinction hierarchies of the American Tianxia regardless of the fact that China is not a democracy. Even individuals who are unable to travel to the United States itself are embedded in US-centered distinction hierarchies. That is part of what makes the American Tianxia universal, despite its geographical limits. It works through states, where those states are sympathetically aligned. Where they are not, it turns directly to their people.

The power that the structure of the American Tianxia gives to its central state thus runs much deeper than mere "soft power." Nye's soft power concept is entirely state-centric (Nye, 1990, pp. 166-168; 2004, pp. 256-261); it is a form of co-optive power: "getting others to want what you want" (Nye, 1990, p. 167) or "the ability to get what you want through attraction rather than coercion or payments" (Nye, 2004, p. 256), where the operative "you" is a state. Thus in Nye's view soft power can be "squandered" through unpopular leadership; he points to occasions on which Presidents George H.W. Bush (Nye, 1990, p. 170) and George W. Bush (Nye, 2004, p. 259) "squandered" US soft power. Nye (2004, pp. 256-260) goes so far as to ridicule those who lightly dismiss the importance of popularity and attractiveness. But he does not go far enough. The ultimate power that the United States derives from the existence of the American Tianxia is network power: "the ability to get what you want by shaping the network opportunities that are available to others."

People want to succeed in global systems of distinction, and the United States has an inordinate ability to shape outcomes in those systems. This is plainly visible in the US use of financial and travel sanctions, but it is much more broadly true. Moreover, the determinative influence of US institutions extends far beyond the borders of the United States. Higher education provides a particularly clear example. Of course, the world's top universities on every international ranking scale are concentrated not just in the West, but in the Anglo-Saxon core of the American Tianxia. But even universities that are not internationally ranked strongly prefer to hire professors who earned their PhDs from top Anglo-Saxon universities. They seek accreditation from US accrediting bodies. They model their curriculums on those of top US universities, often partnering with US or UK universities as paid consultants. They give their professors bonuses for publishing in English-language journals and pay for them to present papers at US conferences. Put simply, they seek distinction within the US-centered global university distinction hierarchy. The network externalities of being part of the US-centered world-system are so overwhelming that no other system really matters.

From *guojia* to *tianxia*

The American Tianxia is a world-system on a global scale, a successor to the modern world-system of c.1500–2000 that, in recognition of its inauguration date, might be called the millennial world-system (Babones, forthcoming). How long this new system will survive is anyone's guess, but where world-systems are concerned the "width of a time point" is measured in centuries, not years or decades. Wallerstein's "long sixteenth century" marked the transition from multiple feudal world-systems of Europe, China, India, and the Americas into a single, global, modern world-system. From the late fifteenth century voyages of Columbus and da Gama to the 1648 Peace of Westphalia that transition took a century and a half to consolidate into the form we recognize today. Similarly, the consolidation of the millennial world-system around the world's new central state took most of a century, from before World War I to the late 1990s. The "American century" was a messy transitional phase, not a final system configuration.

Future analysts looking for a symbolic starting date to match the modern world-system's 1648 are likely to zero in on September 11, 2001. It was on that date that US leaders of all kinds, first and foremost President George W. Bush but going right down the line to academic, business, and civil society leaders, nakedly expounded the message "you are either with us or against us." From Barack Obama's Nobel speech ("I ... reserve the right to act unilaterally if necessary") to Donald Trump's inauguration ("From this moment on, it's going to be America first"), US leaders both left and right have embraced the reality that genuine multilateralism is a dead letter. In the structure of the millennial world-system, the United States is not a country like other countries, nor is it merely Madeleine Albright's "indispensable nation." It is the central state of a new, but not unprecedented world-system. As the political scientist Yuen Foong Khong puts it:

In his superb analysis of the Chinese world order and how it collapsed in the face of Western pressures, Yongjin Zhang honed in on a vocabulary change that revealed China's existential dilemma after the mid-19th century: China's sense of its place in the world shrank from "*tianxia*" (all under heaven) to "*guojia*" (a state), i.e. "the Chinese world became a China in the world." [Zhang, 2001, p. 61] Using the tributary lens to illuminate the *longue durée* of American diplomacy leads one to a rather different conclusion about America's foreign policy trajectory in the 20th and 21st centuries: the United States' place in the world seems to have moved from "*guojia*" to "*tianxia*." (Khong, 2013, p. 42)

From a legal standpoint, the United States is a country like any other, but from a sociological standpoint, the President of the United States is understood to be the "leader of the free world." For Khong (2013, p. 29), this is the telling fact that the United States, its leaders, its public, its foreign policy establishment, and "secondary states" all endorse. There is, in effect, a confluence of US and global power structures in the personality of the President of the United States. It is this confluence that makes so many of the people of the world so uneasy about the personality of Donald Trump.

But it is also this confluence that is responsible for the dramatic reduction in conflict between countries in the postmodern world. The Pax Americana is not rooted in the structure of the interstate system;

even if, like Ming China, the United States were powerful enough to prevent wars between countries, it would have little interest in doing so. The Pax Americana is rooted in the global distinction hierarchies of the American Tianxia. Why should a country's elite want to go to war to expand their country's territory when what they really want is for their children to get into a good university? The most effective way for elite citizens of disadvantaged countries to increase their power and wealth is not make their own countries more powerful and wealthy. It is to leave.

By transferring status competition from the country level to the individual level, the American Tianxia has neutered the nation-state. Countries are still very important as units of local administration, as are provinces, cities, and districts. But their states are no longer the main actors on the historical stage. States do a lot, but they don't make history.

At least, not civilized states. There will always be barbarians at the gates, Fukuyama's (1989, p. 18) "states still caught in the grip of history," and they may cause problems for other states, for their citizens, and for themselves. But for most of the rest of the world, and more specifically for the millennial world-system as a whole, history as we have known it in the West – history as the constant vying of politically-organized human communities for power and prestige – is in hiatus. Politically-organized human communities like nation-states and empires still exist, but they no longer make the running in the global competition for power and prestige. Other forms of human organization are much more relevant.

Hegel saw the end of history (in both normative and chronological terms) as the development of freedom. For Khong (2013, p. 29), the creed of freedom is "what uniquely qualifies the United States to lead." He's right. The United States is a large and powerful state, but as a state it is nowhere near as predominant in the millennial world-system as Ming China was in the pre-modern East Asian world-system. The United States is only able to act as the central state of a global *tianxia* because it has successfully disaggregated the world into individuals. For this it was uniquely (one might say fortuitously) prepared by its founding focus on "Life, Liberty, and the pursuit of Happiness." The US Declaration of Independence takes it for granted – literally, by God – that governments are created by people "to secure these rights" for individuals. In the American tradition, states don't grant rights to people; people create states to secure rights for themselves.

Any state might have ended up the central state of the global world-system, or none. In the sixteenth century it might have been Spain, with control of half of Europe and most of the Americas. In the nineteenth century it might have been Britain, with control of half the world. In the twentieth century it might have been the Soviet Union, or (God forbid) Hitler's Germany. But none of these states could have held the system together for very long, because none of these states held any appeal beyond sheer force, and none of them ever had enough sheer force to bind the rest of the system to itself. In any case, as demonstrated by the histories of China and Rome alike, binding the system through sheer force requires a constant dissipation of energy. For a while that energy can be obtained through ever more repressive exploitation, but ultimately "the empire, long united, must divide." Entropy always wins.

Only a state founded on the primacy of the individual and ideologically committed to freedom of opportunity for all individuals could succeed as the central state of a truly global world-system. The United States is a relatively large state with a relatively large economy, but it doesn't have to be overwhelmingly large because it doesn't have to coerce people into its system. Quite the contrary: there is a long waiting list for admission to the system. The United States doesn't subsidize English language schools, doesn't force people to use the US dollar, doesn't insist that countries adopt its educational practices, doesn't recruit slave labor (any more), and most of all doesn't demand tribute. What it does do is make available to individuals opportunities that their own countries can't or won't provide. The result is an extraordinarily stable central state system in which individuals, especially elite individuals, insist on the maintenance of free access to the US-centered global system as the cornerstone of their own country's national policies.

This wasn't the case in 1917, or even in 1945. There is far too much rose-tinted nostalgia for a mythical post-war order of free trade, multilateral cooperation, and unquestioned American hegemony. The reality of the post-war period was much more sanguinary and much less sanguine. All that ended in the 1990s. After a century of systemic uncertainty and horrific atrocities, the millennial world-system finally solidified into an unprecedented political-economic system based on the network power held by a central state over the personal opportunities for self-advancement of hundreds of millions (if not billions) of citizens of other countries. Whether this is good, bad, or tragic depends on one's perspective. But there is every reason to believe it is stable.

International relations scholars have written extensively about the failed hegemonic transition of 1914, when British hegemony was supposedly challenged by Germany, the later successful hegemonic transition of 1945, when the United States is supposed to have answered the call of destiny, and the twenty-first century hegemonic transition, during which China will supposedly challenge the United States for global supremacy. These scholars – one might say their entire profession – have no sense of the width of a time point. The real system transition lasted an entire century (from c.1900-2000) and has only recently been completed. The century of transition was bloody, repressive (on all sides), and disorderly. It is now over, and the next system transition is likely to be several centuries away.

The millennial world-system and its governance mechanism, the American Tianxia, stand every chance of being more peaceful, more open, and more orderly than the previous modern world-system and its governance mechanism, the anarchic interstate system. Most international relations scholars are still living in the old system and many of them seem to be yearning for the old wars. Meanwhile the new system has its own injustices. Fighting them may prove equally as difficult as fighting the wars of the last system. But with any luck the world will have centuries of boredom before history gets started once again. Contra Fukuyama, it is impossible to be anything but optimistic.

References

Arrighi, G. (2007) *Adam Smith in Beijing: Lineages of the twenty-first century*, London: Verso.

Atwell, W.S. (1982) 'International bullion flows and the Chinese economy circa 1530-1650', *Past and Present*, 95: 68-90.

Atwell, W.S. (1998) 'Ming China and the emerging world economy, c. 1470-1650', in D. Twitchett and F.W. Mote (eds) *The Cambridge History of China, Volume 8: The Ming dynasty, part 2: 1368–1644*, Cambridge: Cambridge University Press, pp. 376-416.

Babones, S. (2011) 'The middling kingdom: The hype and the reality of China's rise', *Foreign Affairs*, 90(5): 79-88.

Babones, S. (2012) 'A structuralist perspective on economic growth in China and India: Anticipating the end game', *International Journal of Sociology and Social Policy*, 32(1/2): 29-41.

Babones, S. (2015a) 'The once and future hegemon', *The National Interest*, 138: 54-62.

Babones, S. (2015b) 'Russia's eastern gambit', *Russia in Global Affairs*, 13(3): 131-141.

Babones, S. (2015c) 'Two little, too late: China's one child policy and population collapse', *Foreign Affairs* online: November 12.

Babones, S. (2015d) 'What "is" world-systems analysis? Distinguishing theory from perspective', *Thesis Eleven*, 127: 3-20.

Babones, S. (2016) 'How weak is China? The real story behind the economic indicators', *Foreign Affairs* online: January 31.

Babones, S. (2017a) 'The new geography of the global economy: Brexit as Amerentry', *Quadrant*, 61(3): 12–15.

Babones, S. (2017b) 'Sovereignty in the millennial world-system', in A. Bergesen and C. Suter (eds) *The Return of Geopolitics*, Berlin: Lit Verlag.

Beard, C.A. (1922) *Cross Currents in Europe To-day*, Boston: Marshall Jones.

Bell, D.A. (2008) *China's new Confucianism: Politics and everyday life in a changing society*, Princeton, NJ: Princeton University Press.

Ben Naceur, S., Hosny, A., and Hadjian, G. (2015) *How to De-dollarize Financial Systems in the Caucasus and Central Asia?*, Washington, DC: International Monetary Fund.

Bolt, J. and van Zanden, J.L. (2014) 'The Maddison Project: Collaborative research on historical national accounts', *Economic History Review*, 67(3): 627–651.

Bond, P. (2010) 'BRICS and the sub-imperial location', in P. Bond and A. Garcia (eds) *BRICS: An anti-capitalist critique*, Aukland Park: Jacana Media, pp. 15-26.

Brooks, S.G. and Wohlforth, W.C. (2016a) *America Abroad: The United States' global role in the 21st century*, Oxford: Oxford University Press.

Brooks, S.G. and Wohlforth, W.C. (2016b) 'The rise and fall of the great powers in the twenty-first century: China's rise and the fate of America's global position', *International Security*, 40(3): 7-53.

Bull, H. (1977) *The Anarchical Society: A study of order in world politics*, 4th ed, London: Macmillan.

Busse, M., Erdogan, C., and Muhlen, H. (2016) 'China's impact on Africa - The role of trade, FDI and aid', *KYKLOS*, 69(2): 228-262.

Callahan, W.A. (2004) 'Remembering the future: Utopia, empire, and harmony in 21st-century international theory', *European Journal of International Relations*, 10(4): 569-601.

Callahan, W.A. (2012) 'China's strategic futures: Debating the post-American world order', *Asian Survey*, 52(4): 617-642.

Callahan, W.A. (2014) 'Chinese exceptionalism and the politics of history', in N. Horesh and E. Kavalski (eds) *Asian Thought on China's Changing International Relations*, New York: Palgrave Macmillan, pp. 17-33.

Census Bureau (2017) *International data base*, Washington, DC: US Census Bureau.

CGTN (2015) 'Chinese fertility rate drops into "low fertility trap"', Beijing: CGTN.

Chan, H.L. (1968) 'The "Chinese barbarian officials" in the foreign tributary missions to China during the Ming Dynasty', *Journal of the American Oriental Society*, 88(3): 411–418.

Chang, C.S. (2011) 'Tianxia system on a snail's horns', *Inter-Asia Cultural Studies*, 12(1): 28–42.

Chanlett-Avery, E. and Rinehart, I.E. (2016) *The U.S. Military Presence in Okinawa and the Futenma Base Controversy*, Washington, DC: Congressional Research Service.

Chase-Dunn, C.K. (1998) *Global Formation: Structures of the world-economy*, updated ed, Lanham, MD: Rowman and Littlefield.

Chen, Z.M. and Pan, Z.Q. (2011) 'China in its neighbourhood: A "middle kingdom" not necessarily at the centre of power', *The International Spectator*, 46(4): 79–96.

Clarke, M. (2014) 'Kazakh responses to the rise of China: Between elite bandwagoning and societal ambivalence?', in N. Horesh and E. Kavalski (eds) *Asian Thought on China's Changing International Relations*, New York: Palgrave Macmillan, pp. 141–172.

Constantaras, E. (2016) 'Visualizing China's aid to Africa: China aid map reveals nearly $100 billion infrastructure investment boom in Africa', *ChinaFile* online, June 30.

Croxton, D. (1999) 'The Peace of Westphalia of 1648 and the origins of sovereignty', *International History Review*, 21(3): 569–591.

Curcuru, S.E., Thomas, C.P., and Warnock F.E. (2013) 'On returns differentials', *Journal of International Money and Finance*, 36: 1–25.

Dadush, U. and Stancil, B. (2010), *The World Order in 2050*, Washington, DC: Carnegie Endowment for International Peace.

Demieville, P. (1986) 'Philosophy and religion from Han to Sui', in D. Twitchett and M. Loewe (eds) *The Cambridge History of China, Volume 1: The Ch'in and Han empires, 221 BC–AD 220*, Cambridge: Cambridge University Press, pp. 808–872.

DHS (2016) *2015 Yearbook of Immigration Statistics*, Washington, DC: Department of Homeland Security.

Dubs, H.H. and Smith, R.S. (1942) 'Chinese in Mexico City in 1635', *The Far Eastern Quarterly*, 1(4): 387-438.

Fairbank, J.K. and Teng, S.Y. (1941) 'On the Ch'ing tributary system', *Harvard Journal of Asiatic Studies*, 6(2): 135-246.

Farchy, J. (2016) 'New Silk Road will transport laptops and frozen chicken', *Financial Times* online, May 10.

Feng, H.Y. and He, K. (2015) 'America in the eyes of America watchers: Survey research in Beijing in 2012', *Journal of Contemporary China*, 24(91): 83-100.

Feng, Z.P. and Huang, J. (2014) *China's Strategic Partnership Diplomacy: Engaging with a changing world*, Brussels: European Strategic Partnerships Observatory.

Ferdinand, P. (2016) 'Westward ho - The China dream and "one belt, one road": Chinese foreign policy under Xi Jinping', *International Affairs*, 92(4): 941–957.

Flynn, D.O. and Giraldez, A. (1995) 'Born with a "silver spoon": The origin of world trade in 1571', *Journal of World History*, 6(2): 201-221.

Fogel, R. (2010) '$123,000,000,000,000★: ★China's estimated economy by the year 2040. Be warned', *Foreign Policy*, 177: 70-75.

FRED (2017) *FRED economic data* database, St. Louis, MO: Federal Reserve Bank of St. Louis.

Fukuyama, F. (1989) 'The end of history?', *The National Interest*, 16: 3-18.

Fukuyama, F. (1992) *The End of History and the Last Man*, New York: Free Press.

Fukuyama, F. (1995) 'Reflections on the end of history, five years later', *History and Theory*, 34(2): 27-43.

Fukuyama, F. (2007) 'The history at the end of history', *Guardian* online, April 3.

Goodman, D.S.G. (2004) 'The campaign to "Open Up the West": National, provincial-level and local perspectives', *China Quarterly*, 178: 317-334.

Gordon, P. and Morales Del Pino, J.J. (2017) *The Silver Way: China, Spanish America and the birth of globalisation, 1565–1815*, New York: Penguin.

Gunter, F.R. (2017) 'Corruption, costs, and family: Chinese capital flight, 1984-2014', *China Economic Review*, 43: 105-117.

Hackenesch, C. (2013) 'Aid donor meets strategic partner? The European Union's and China's relations with Ethiopia', *Journal of Current Chinese Affairs*, 42(1): 7–36.

Harvey, D. (2003) *The New Imperialism*, Oxford: Oxford University Press.

Hearn, A. (2016) *Diaspora and Trust: Cuba, Mexico, and the rise of China*, Durham, NC: Duke University Press.

Hegel, G.W.F. (1861) *Lectures on the Philosophy of History*, 3rd ed (J. Sirbee, tr), London: Henry G. Bohn.

Hess, S. and Aidoo, R. (2015) *Charting the Roots of Anti-Chinese Populism in Africa*, New York: Springer.

Heydarian, R.J. (2015) *Asia's New Battlefield: The USA, China and the struggle for the Western Pacific*, London: Zed Books.

Hoe, S. and Roebuck, D. (1999) *The Taking of Hong Kong: Charles and Clara Elliot in China waters*, Oxford: Routledge.

Hopkin, J. and Blyth, M. (2014) 'Londongrad calling: The United Kingdom's dangerous dependence on Russian money', *Foreign Affairs* online, April 21.

Hsu, S. (2017) 'How China's Asian Infrastructure Investment Bank fared its first year', *Forbes* online, January 14.

Huang, C.C. and Shih, C.Y. (2014) *Harmonious Intervention: China's quest for relational security*, Farnham: Ashgate.

Huang, Y., Tang, W., Mu, Y., Li, X.H., Liu, Z., Wang, Y.P., Li, M.G., Li, Q., Dai, L., Liang, J., and Zhu, J. (2016) 'The sex ratio at birth for 5,338,853 deliveries in China from 2012 to 2015: A facility-based study', *PLoS ONE*, 11(12): e0167575.

Huang, Y.Z. (2016) 'China's new two child policy: Too little, too late', *Asia Unbound* blog, New York: Council on Foreign Relations.

Hucker, C.O. (1998) 'Ming government', in D. Twitchett and F.W. Mote (eds) *The Cambridge History of China, Volume 8: The Ming dynasty, part 2: 1368–1644*, Cambridge: Cambridge University Press, pp. 9-105.

Hutt, D. (2016) 'How China came to dominate Cambodia: How Cambodia went from denouncing China to being Beijing's most faithful client state', *The Diplomat* online, September 1.

Institute of International Finance (2017) *February 2017 Capital Flows to Emerging Markets*, Washington, DC: Institute of International Finance.

Jacques, M. (2009) *When China Rules the World: The end of the Western world and the birth of a new global order*, New York: Penguin.

Jiang, Y.L. (2011) *The Mandate of Heaven and* The Great Ming Code, Seattle, WA: University of Washington Press.

Kang, D.C. (2010) *East Asia before the West: Five centuries of trade and tribute*, New York: Columbia University Press.

Kern, M. (2010). 'Early Chinese literature, beginnings through Western Han', in K.S. Chang and S. Owen (eds) *The Cambridge History of Chinese Literature, Volume 1: To 1375*, Cambridge: Cambridge University Press, pp. 1-115.

Khong, Y.F. (2013) 'The American tributary system', *The Chinese Journal of International Politics*, 6(1): 1-47.

Koga, K. (2016) 'The rise of China and Japan's balancing strategy: Critical junctures and policy shifts in the 2010s', *Journal of Contemporary China*, 25(101): 777-791.

Kojeve, A. (1969) *Introduction to the reading of Hegel: Lectures on the phenomenology of spirit*, Ithaca, NY: Cornell University Press.

Krasner, S.D. (1999) *Sovereignty: Organized hypocrisy*, Princeton, NJ: Princeton University Press.

Krauthammer, C. (1990) 'The unipolar moment', *Foreign Affairs*, 70(1): 23-33.

Lai, H.Y.H. (2002) 'China's Western Development Program: Its rationale, implementation, and prospects', *Modern China*, 28(4): 432-466.

Layne, C. (1993) 'The unipolar illusion: Why new great powers will rise', *International Security*, 17(4): 5-51.

Layne, C. (2006) 'The unipolar illusion revisited: The coming end of the United States' unipolar moment', *International Security*, 31(2): 7–41.

Liff, A.P. and Ikenberry, G.J. (2014) 'Racing toward tragedy? China's rise, military competition in the Asia Pacific, and the security dilemma', *International Security*, 39(2): 52-91.

Lockard, C.A. (2013) 'Chinese migration and settlement in Southeast Asia before 1850: Making fields from the sea', *History Compass*, 11(9): 765-781.

Luce, H.R. (1941) 'The American century', *Life*, February 17: 61-65.

Luo, Z.T. (2008) 'From "tianxia" (all under heaven) to "the world": Changes in late Qing intellectuals' conceptions of human society', *Social Sciences in China*, 24(2): 93-105.

Lynch, D.C. (2015) *China's Futures: PRC elites debate economics, politics, and foreign policy*, Stanford, CA: Stanford University Press.

Mackinder, H.J. (1904) 'The geographical pivot of history', *Geographical Journal*, 23(4): 421-437.

Mackinder, H.J. (1919) *Democratic Ideals and Reality: A study in the politics of reconstruction*, London: Henry Holt.

Mahoney, J.G. (2008) 'On the way to harmony: Marxism, Confucianism, and Hu Jintao's *hexie* concept', in S.J. Guo and B.G. Guo (eds) *China in Search of a Harmonious Society*, Lanham, MD: Lexington Books, pp. 99-128.

Mancall, M. (1971) *Russia and China: Their diplomatic relations to 1728*, Cambridge, MA: Harvard University Press.

Manyin, M.E., Chanlett-Avery, E., Nikitin, M.B.D., Williams, B.R., and Corrado, J.R. (2016) *U.S.–South Korea relations*, Washington, DC: Congressional Research Service.

Mauch, P. (2014) 'Japanese intellectual responses to China's rise', in N. Horesh and E. Kavalski (eds) *Asian Thought on China's Changing International Relations*, New York: Palgrave Macmillan, pp. 192-204.

McCauley, R.N. (2015) 'Does the US dollar confer an exorbitant privilege?', *Journal of International Money and Finance*, 57: 1-14.

McGann, J.G. (2016) *2015 Global go to Think Tank Index Report*, Philadelphia, PA: University of Pennsylvania Scholarly Commons.

Mearsheimer, J.J. (1990) 'Back to the future: Instability in Europe after the Cold War', *International Security*, 15(1): 5-56.

Menon, S. (2016) 'China, the world and India', *China Report*, 52(2): 129-137.

Meyer, J.W., Boli, J., Thomas, G.M., and Ramirez, F.O. (1997) 'World society and the nation-state', *American Journal of Sociology*, 103(1): 144-181.

Morris, I. (2014) *War! What is it good for? The role of conflict in civilization from primates to robots*, New York: Farrar, Straus, and Giroux.

National Bureau of Statistics (2016) *China Statistical Yearbook 2016* database, Beijing: National Bureau of Statistics.

Nye, J.S., Jr. (1990) 'Soft power', *Foreign Policy*, 80: 153-171.

Nye, J.S., Jr. (2004) 'Soft power and American foreign policy', *Political Science Quarterly*, 119(2): 255-270.

Nye, J.S., Jr. (2015) *Is the American Century Over?*, Cambridge: Policy Press.

Nye, J.S., Jr. (2017) 'Will the liberal order survive? The history of an idea', *Foreign Affairs*, 96(1): 10-16.

O'Sullivan, J. (2006) *The President, the Pope, and the Prime Minister: Three who changed the world*, Washington, DC: Regnery Publishing.

Pan, S.Y. and Lo, J.T.Y. (2017) 'Re-conceptualizing China's rise as a global power: A neo-tributary perspective', *Pacific Review*, 30(1): 1-25.

People's Daily (2016) 'China's population will be down to half by the end of this century?', *People's Daily* online, June 30.

Perdue, P.C. (2015) 'The tenacious tributary system', *Journal of Contemporary China*, 24(96): 1002-1014.

Peyrouse, S. (2016) 'Discussing China: Sinophilia and Sinophobia in Central Asia', *Journal of Eurasian Studies*, 7(1): 14-23.

Pinker, S. (2011) *The Better Angels of our Nature: Why violence has declined*, New York: Viking Books.

Qi, H.G. and Shen, D.L. (2015) 'Chinese traditional world citizenship thoughts and its impact on the cultivation of Chinese world citizenship awareness', *Citizenship Studies*, 19(3-4): 267-284.

Qin, Y.Q. (2011) 'Rule, rules, and relations: Towards a synthetic approach to governance', *Chinese Journal of International Politics*, 4(2): 117-145.

Qin, Y.Q. (2012) 'Culture and global thought: Chinese international theory in the making', *Revista CIDOB d'Afers Internacionals*, 100: 67-89.

Raymo, J.M., Park, H.J., Xie, Y., and Yeung, Y.J.J. (2015) 'Marriage and family in East Asia: continuity and change', *Annual Review of Sociology*, 41: 471-492.

Roy, D. (2016) 'Meeting the Chinese challenge to the regional order', *Asian Politics & Policy*, 8(1): 193-206.

Rumer, E., Sokolsky, R., and Stronski, P. (2016) *US Policy toward Central Asia 3.0*, Washington: Carnegie Endowment for International Peace.

Russell, B. and Russell, D. (1923) *The Prospects of Industrial Civilization*, London: Allen & Unwin.

Schweller, R.L. and Pu, X.Y. (2011) 'After unipolarity: China's visions of international order in an era of U.S. decline', *International Security*, 36(1): 41-72.

Sheehan, M. (2015) 'Born in the USA: Why Chinese 'birth tourism' is booming in California', *The World Post* online, May 1.

Smith, D.L. (1996) 'Central Asia: A new Great Game?', *Asian Affairs*, 23(3): 147-175.

Starrs, S. (2013) 'American economic power hasn't declined – it globalized! Summoning the data and taking globalization seriously', *International Studies Quarterly*, 57(4): 817-830.

Sun, Y. (2014a) *Africa in China's Foreign Policy*, Washington, DC: Brookings Institution.

Sun, Y. (2014b) 'Africa in China's new foreign aid white paper', *Brookings Africa in Focus* online, July 16.

Swanstrom, N. (2005) 'China and Central Asia: A new Great Game or traditional vassal relations?', *Journal of Contemporary China*, 14(45): 569–584.

Tow, W.T. and Limaye, S. (2016) 'What's China got to do with it? U.S. alliances, partnerships in the Asia-Pacific', *Asian Politics & Policy*, 8(1): 7–26.

Tsiang, T.F. (1936) 'China and European expansion', *Politica*, 2(5): 1–18.

UNPD (2015) *2015 Revision of World Population Prospects*, New York: United Nations Population Division.

Vine, D. (2015) *Base Nation: How U.S. military bases abroad harm America and the world*, New York: Metropolitan Books.

Wade, G. (2005) 'The Zheng He voyages: A reassessment', *Journal of the Malaysian Branch of the Royal Asiatic Society*, 8(1): 37–58.

Wallerstein, I.M. (1974) *The Modern World-System: Capitalist agriculture and the origins of the European world-economy in the sixteenth century*, New York: Academic Press.

Wang, G.W. (1959) *A Short History of the Nanyang Chinese*, Singapore: Eastern Universities Press.

Wang, G.W. (1968) 'Early Ming relations with Southeast Asia: A background essay', in J. Fairbank (ed) *The Chinese World Order: Traditional China's foreign relations*, Cambridge, MA: Harvard University Press, pp. 34–62.

Wang, G.W. (1998) 'Ming foreign relations: Southeast Asia', in D. Twitchett and F.W. Mote (eds) *The Cambridge History of China, Volume 8: The Ming dynasty, part 2: 1368–1644*, Cambridge: Cambridge University Press, pp. 301–332.

Wang, G.W. (2013) *Renewal: The Chinese state and the new global history*, Hong Kong: Chinese University Press.

Weitz, R. (2006) 'Averting a new great game in Central Asia', *The Washington Quarterly*, 29(3): 155–167.

Wheaton, H. (1836) *Elements of International Law with a Sketch of the History of the Science*, Philadelphia: Carey, Lea, and Blanchard.

Willis, J.E. (1998) 'Relations with maritime Europeans, 1514–1662', in D. Twitchett and F.W. Mote (eds) *The Cambridge History of China, Volume 8: The Ming dynasty, part 2: 1368–1644*, Cambridge: Cambridge University Press, pp. 333–375.

Wohlforth, W.C. (1999) 'The stability of a unipolar world', *International Security*, 24(1): 5–41.

World Bank (2016) *World Development Indicators* database, Washington, DC: World Bank.

Xiang, B. (2016) *Emigration Trends and Policies in China: Movement of the wealthy and highly skilled*, Washington, DC: Migration Policy Institute.

Xu, J. (2016) 'Debates in IR academia and China's policy adjustments', *Chinese Journal of International Politics*, 9(4): 459–485.

Yan, X.T. (2001) 'The rise of China in China's eyes', *Journal of Contemporary China*, 10(26): 33–39.

Yan, X.T. (2014) 'From keeping a low profile to striving for achievement', *Chinese Journal of International Politics*, 7(2): 153–184.

Yu, Y.S. (1986) 'Han foreign relations', in D. Twitchett and M. Loewe (eds) *The Cambridge History of China, Volume 1: The Ch'in and Han empires, 221 BC–AD 220*, Cambridge: Cambridge University Press, pp. 377–462.

Zhang, F. (2009) 'Rethinking the "tribute system": Broadening the conceptual horizon of historical East Asian politics', *Chinese Journal of International Politics*, 2(4): 545–574.

Zhang, F. (2010) 'The *tianxia* system: World order in a Chinese utopia', *Global Asia*, 4(4): 108–112.

Zhang, F. (2015a) *Chinese Hegemony: Grand strategy and international institutions in East Asian History*, Stanford, CA: Stanford University Press.

Zhang, Y.J. (2001) 'System, empire and state in Chinese international relations', *Review of International Studies*, 27(5): 43–63.

Zhang, Y.J. and Buzan, B. (2012) 'The tributary system as international society in theory and practice', *Chinese Journal of International Politics*, 5(1): 3–36.

Zhang, Y.L. (2015b) 'One Belt, One Road: A Chinese view', *Global Asia*, 10(3): 8-12.

Zhao, T.Y. (2006) 'Rethinking empire from a Chinese concept "all-under-heaven" (tian-xia)', *Social Identities*, 12(1): 29-41.

Zhao, T.Y. (2009) 'A political world philosophy in terms of all-under-heaven (tian-xia)', *Diogenes*, 221: 5-18.

Zhao, T.Y. (2012) 'All-under-heaven and methodological relationalism: An old story and new world peace', in F. Dallmayr and T.Y. Zhao (eds) *Contemporary Chinese Political Thought: Debates and perspectives*, Lexington: University Press of Kentucky, pp. 46-66.

Zhao, K.J. (2015) 'The motivation behind China's public diplomacy', *Chinese Journal of International Politics*, 8(2): 167-196.

Zheng, Y.N. and Wu, D. (2014) 'Wang Gungwu and the study of China's international relations', in N. Horesh and E. Kavalski (eds) *Asian Thought on China's Changing International Relations*, New York: Palgrave Macmillan, pp. 54-75.

Zizek, S. (2011) *Living in the End Times*, London: Verso.

Index

Printed and bound by CPI Group (UK) Ltd, Croydon, CR0 4YY

13/04/2025

14656588-0001